HENRY VIII

Henry VIII of England (1491–1547, king from 1509 to 1547). Perhaps the most memorable and commonly known image of the king, and a painting copied by countless artists. The original was by Hans Holbein the Younger. Royal Collection

HENRY VIII

THE EVOLUTION OF A REPUTATION

KEITH DOCKRAY
AND ALAN SUTTON

FONTHILL

The historian and the publisher: Keith Dockray and Alan Sutton at the Château de Chinon.

Front cover illustration: Detail from a portrait of Henry VIII by the workshop of Hans Holbein the Younger, (1537–1540). *Walker Art Gallery*

Back cover illustration: Portrait of Henry VIII by Hans Holbein the Younger, *c.* 1537. *Thyssen-Bornemisza Museum, Madrid*

Fonthill Media Limited
Fonthill Media LLC
www.fonthillmedia.com
office@fonthillmedia.com

First published in the United Kingdom
and the United States of America 2016

British Library Cataloguing in Publication Data:
A catalogue record for this book is available from the British Library

Copyright © Keith Dockray and Alan Sutton 2016

ISBN 978-1-78155-533-0

Typeset in Minion Pro 11pt on 15pt
Printed and bound by CPI Group (UK) Ltd, Croydon, CR0 4YY

Contents

Henry VIII *c.* 1530–1535. The Latin inscription on the scroll translates into English as: 'Go ye into all the world, and preach the gospel to every creature' (Mark 16:15). A painting by Joos van Cleve, (*c.* 1485–1541). *Royal Collection*

The Family of Henry VIII. The immediate family members portrayed are the Lady Mary, Prince Edward, Henry VIII, Jane Seymour and the Lady Elizabeth. The female character in the doorway to the left is a matter of some doubt; it is now usually believed she is Jane the Fool, but, if not, she may be Mother Jak, who had possibly been a wet nurse to Prince Edward as an infant. More confidently, the male character in the door way to the right is Will Sommers (or Wil Somers), the best-known court jester of Henry VIII. Unknown artist, *c.* 1545. *Royal Collection, Hampton Court Palace*

Preface

THIS LIGHT-HEARTED SURVEY OF THE historiography of Henry VIII was originally penned, in 2010, as the introductory section of a never completed biography of the second Tudor king. Early in 2013, despite its unsuitability for inclusion in a volume of traditional academic history papers, I sent a copy to Linda Clark as a possible contribution to a festschrift in honour of eminent fifteenth-century historian Michael Hicks. Inevitably, it was politely declined for the volume but Linda did send an edited version to Michael (who, apparently, enjoyed reading it), as well as encouraging me to secure its formal publication as a booklet. Long-time friend Alan Sutton, founder of Fonthill Media Limited, generously took on the task and here is the result!

Keith Dockray
Bristol
September 2015

Illustrations

ONVENTION IN ENGLISH HISTORY SEEMS to have created a dividing line, at 1485, between later medieval and early modern eras. There is good reason for this as the last of the Plantagenets, Richard III, lost his throne on the Bosworth battlefield to Henry VII, first of the Tudors. This neatly coincides, moreover, with the flowering of the Renaissance in England; the onset of the Reformation soon followed; and, at the same time, came the revolutionary impact of printing. Portraiture particularly flourished, and indeed, crashed through a real barrier with the emergence of accurate visual perspective (most notably at Henry VIII's court in the work of Hans Holbein the Younger). No less significantly, for the first time in history, printed woodcuts enabled illustrations to be mass produced.

As a result we have been able to include a range of illustrations in the text here, among them portrayals of historians, as well as a Henrician Gallery of further visual material at the end of the volume in very approximate chronological sequence. The vast majority of the images are in the public domain but, where known, we have provided information about the location of originals. Needless to say, we apologise sincerely if we have inadvertently breached any copyrights.

Alan has devoted so much time to this booklet, especially selecting appropriate illustrations and penning informative captions, that I have insisted on its being published under both our names.

Keith Dockray
November 2015

Henry VII, Elizabeth of York, Henry VIII, and Jane Seymour. A painting by Remigius van Leemput, (1607–1675). This painting was commissioned by Charles II, and fortunately so, for the original on which it was based was destroyed by fire. The original was a mural in the Palace of Whitehall by Hans Holbein the Younger, lost when the palace burned down on 4 January 1698, and this is the only complete copy. *Royal Collection, Windsor Castle*

Introduction

No English king is more famous—or infamous!—than Henry VIII. He is remembered, in particular, as the formidable and arrogant regal figure portrayed by Hans Holbein the Younger, the early Tudor stud who clocked up no fewer than six wives, and the proto-nationalist/imperialist ruler who sent the pope packing and inaugurated the English Reformation. Nor is it easy to avoid contrasting the handsome, athletic and affable teenage prince who ascended the throne in 1509 with the bloated, physically decrepit and irritable elderly king he had become by the time of his death in 1547. As befits such a colossus, moreover, masses has been written about Henry VIII, not only by contemporary and near-contemporary commentators but also professional and amateur historians (and historical novelists!) ever since. Verdicts have varied enormously and extremes of interpretation are not difficult to find. In the early seventeenth-century, indeed, the wise, virtuous, benevolent and majestic king portrayed in *Henry VIII* (a play traditionally ascribed to William Shakespeare) seems to be almost entirely a product of the playwright's own fertile imagination. No less fancifully, if in complete contrast, the nineteenth-century novelist Charles Dickens felt moved to comment on this 'most intolerable ruffian, a disgrace to human nature, and a blot of blood and grease on the History of England'. When penning their classic spoof *1066 and All That* in 1930, moreover, W. C. Sellar and R. J. Yeatman had no problem at all in lampooning 'Bluff King Hal' as 'a strong king with a very strong sense of humour' (albeit only too apparently warped in the game where his ministers, 'blindfolded and knelt down with their heads on a block of wood', were invited to guess whom the king would marry next); a well-developed taste for both tennis and diplomacy (not least when he met 'the young King of France in a field called the Field of the Crock of Gold'); and the husband of not six but 'VIII wives, memorable amongst whom were Katherine the Arrogant, Anne of Cloves, Lady Jane Austin, and Anne Hathaway'. And as for John Farman, whose sardonic *Very Bloody History of Britain* was published in 1990, he simply concluded that the 'world-famous Henry VIII', an 'all-round clever Dick' if ever there was one in 1509, had so degenerated physically by 1547 that his appalling afflictions are just too disgusting to recall!

Even in his own lifetime Henry VIII's contemporaries brought in contrasting verdicts: a Venetian envoy in 1515, for instance, concluded that the king was 'the handsomest potentate I ever set eyes on' and 'in every respect a most accomplished prince'; yet, in 1540, a French ambassador reported very differently on a monarch who, by then, had become so covetous and suspicious of those around him that 'every day edicts are published so sanguinary that even with a thousand guards one would scarce be safe'. A few decades later, in 1614, Sir Walter Raleigh declared himself convinced that, even if 'all the pictures and patterns of a merciless prince were lost to the world, they might all again be painted to the life out of the story' of Henry VIII; in 1679, while Bishop Gilbert Burnet could not deny the king a place 'among ill princes', he felt equally unable to 'rank him with the worst'; and as for David Hume in 1759, he firmly believed that the second Tudor's 'absolute uncontrolled authority' was beyond question. Henry VIII certainly attracted a great deal of frequently

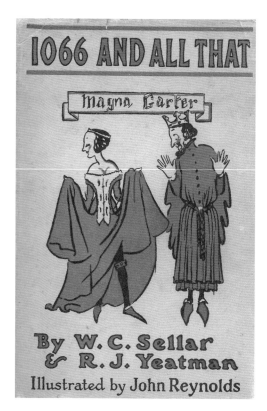

1066 And all That: A Memorable History of England. This unforgettable book, 'the history book to end all history books' by Walter Carruthers Sellar and Robert Julian Yeatman was first published by Methuen & Co. Ltd, London, in 1930. This illustration is from the 1960 edition.

hostile attention from early nineteenth-century Whig historians: Henry Hallam in 1827, for instance, deliberately chose to highlight the king's 'sudden and harsh' innovations in religion, his 'destruction of venerable establishments' and his 'tyranny over the recesses of the conscience', while, for Lord Macaulay in 1848, he was quite simply 'despotism personified'. Yet, according to J. A. Froude a few years later, for all his faults Henry VIII was perhaps 'the greatest of his contemporaries and the man best able, of all living Englishmen, to govern England'. As for Charles Oman in 1895, he could hardly contain his enthusiasm. Henry VIII, he declared, was:

> . . . perhaps the most remarkable man who ever sat upon the English throne. He guided England through the epoch of change and unrest which lay between the middle ages and modern history, and his guidance was of such a peculiar and

personal stamp that he left an indelible mark on the land for
many succeeding generations.

For the king's compelling and influential early twentieth-century
biographer A. F. Pollard, too, Henry was 'the most remarkable man
who ever sat on the English throne'; moreover, he believed, 'no
ruler has ever left a deeper impress on the history of his country'.
J. J Scarisbrick, in another important biography published in 1968,
found him 'a huge, consequential and majestic figure' who 'raised
the monarchy to near-idolatry' and became 'the quintessence of
Englishry and the focus of a swelling national pride'. Yet another
biographer, Jasper Ridley, concluded in 1984 that, 'although
Henry used the services of others and listened to their advice',
he nevertheless 'took all the decisions' himself, 'whether in the
hunting field, at the butts, in the park at Hampton Court, in camp
at Boulogne, or in his sickbed at Whitehall'. And, shortly before the
five hundredth anniversary of Henry VIII's accession to the throne in
1509, the eminent historian-cum-television presenter David Starkey's
in-depth investigations into the king's life and times over many years
inspired one of the most striking judgements ever penned on the
second Tudor and his legacy:

> Henry VIII was Britain's most powerful king and his reign
> dramatically altered the course of English history. An absolute
> monarch, he was a man whose quest for fame was as obsessive
> as that of any modern celebrity. His desperate longing for a
> male heir led him into territory where no previous monarch
> had dared to venture and his fierce battles against papal
> authority mark one of the most dramatic and defining moments
> in the history of Britain. Half a millennium after he lived,
> moreover, this Renaissance prince-turned-tyrant still towers
> over history.

Henry VIII in later years. Although Henry recovered from his 1536 jousting incident, he suffered from serious leg problems which plagued him for the rest of his life. It has also been conjectured that there was an undetected brain injury which profoundly affected his personality. Certainly his medical problems grew worse in his later years, especially his ulcerated legs and his obesity. Measurements of his armour show that, between his twenties and his fifties, the 6 foot 1 inch monarch's waist grew from 32 inches to 52 inches; his chest expanded from 39 inches to 53 inches, and by the time of his death in 1547 at the age of 56 he is likely to have weighed 28 stone, (392 lb or 178 kg). Portrait at Longleat House, Wiltshire. *Courtesy Richard Rex*

The Family of Henry VIII: An Allegory of the Tudor Succession. The inscription shows that the work was a gift for Francis Walsingham, to whose family its provenance can be traced. Painted in Elizabeth's reign *c.* 1572, the picture is anachronistic and allegorical, demonstrating the queen's legitimate Tudor descent. To the right of Henry are Mary and her husband Philip II of Spain; to Henry's left Edward and Elizabeth. A painting attributed to Lucas de Heere, (1534–1584). *National Museum Cardiff*

1

Contemporary and Near-Contemporary Accounts

MANY CONTEMPORARY AND NEAR-CONTEMPORARY COMMENTATORS found Henry VIII an exciting larger-than-life figure and, during his early years on the throne at least, this may well have reflected the king's own enthusiastically projected image of himself, his court and his regal aspirations. Whatever the realities of the case, the young Henry VIII seemed a veritable prince of the Renaissance to his early sixteenth-century subjects: every inch a king, he was handsome, athletic, musical, an accomplished linguist, a patron of the arts and (apparently) a true son of the church; moreover, he combined great charm and affability with enormous self-confidence and tremendous force of character.

Just five weeks after Henry's accession to the throne William Blount Lord Mountjoy, who probably knew the new king better than most, could hardly contain his enthusiasm when writing to the humanist Erasmus of Rotterdam on 27 May 1509:

> I have no fear, my Erasmus, but when you heard that our prince, now Henry the Eighth, whom we may call our Octavius, had succeeded to his father's throne, all your melancholy left you at once. For what may you not promise yourself from a prince, with

whose extraordinary and almost divine character you are well acquainted, and to whom you are not only known but intimate, having received from him a letter traced with his own fingers? But when you know what a hero he now shows himself, how wisely he behaves, what a lover he is of justice and goodness, what affection he bears to the learned, I venture to swear that you will need no wings to make you fly to behold this new and auspicious star. Oh, my Erasmus, if you could see how all the world here is rejoicing in the possession of so great a prince, how his life is all their desire, you could not contain your tears for joy. The heavens laugh, the earth exults, all things are full of milk, of honey and of nectar! Avarice is expelled the country. Liberality scatters wealth with bounteous hand. Our king does not desire gold or gems or precious metals, but virtue, glory, immortality.

Erasmus had first met Henry VIII as long ago as 1499 when, even as a nine year old child, he detected in him 'a certain royal demeanour, a dignity of mind combined with a remarkable courtesy'; as for the king, in 1518 he judged him 'the most sensible monarch of our age' and his 'brilliant' court the 'seat and citadel' of its 'best studies and characters': indeed, he declared, the resulting 'palace' filled with men 'who excel in learning and in prudence' might all too justifiably be dubbed 'a Temple of the Muses rather than a Court'. Similarly, in July 1519, Erasmus again commented approvingly on the king's 'wise desire to surround himself with men of the best, learned, grave, true and honourable', among them England's leading humanist Thomas More. As for More himself, long before losing his head or being in any danger of doing so, he once remarked that:

> . . . the king has a way of making every man feel that he is enjoying his special favour, just as the London wives pray before the image of Our Lady by the Tower till each of them believes it is smiling upon her.

Desiderius Erasmus, (1466–1536). Erasmus was a Dutch Renaissance humanist, Catholic priest, social critic, teacher, and theologian. A painting by Hans Holbein the Younger.

Sir Thomas More, (1478–1535). More was an English lawyer, social philosopher, author, statesman and noted Renaissance humanist. He was a councillor to Henry VIII, and Lord High Chancellor of England, October 1529–16 May 1532. A painting by Hans Holbein the Younger, 1527.

IOANNES HOLPENIVS BA— —SILEENSIS
.SVI IPSIVS EFFIGIATOR. .Æ: XLV.

Hans Holbein the Younger, (c. 1497–1542), A self-portrait. Holbein was born in Augsburg, Bavaria but travelled to England in 1526 in search of work, with a recommendation from Erasmus. He was welcomed into the humanist circle of Thomas More, where he quickly built a high reputation. By 1532 he had obtained the patronage of Anne Boleyn and Thomas Cromwell. By 1535, he was King's Painter to King Henry VIII.

Equally striking (and prophetic!), if we can trust More's son-in-law and biographer William Roper, are words uttered by him after a meeting with the king in 1524/5:

> I find his grace my very good lord indeed, and I believe he doth as singularly favour me as any subject within this realm. However, son Roper, I may tell thee I have no cause to be proud thereof, for if my head could win him a castle in France (for then was there war between us) it should not fail to go.

Venetian envoys to the young Henry VIII's court seem to have been virtually mesmerised by both the king's appearance and his accomplishments. In 1515, for instance, Lorenzo Pasqualigo reported enthusiastically that he was:

. . . above the usual height, with an extremely fine calf to his leg, his complexion very fair and bright, with auburn hair combed straight and short, in the French fashion, and a round face so very beautiful that it would become a pretty woman. . . He speaks French, English and Latin, and a little Italian, plays well on the lute and harpsichord, sings from book at sight, draws the bow with greater strength than any man in England, and jousts marvellously.

In similar vein another Italian diplomat, Sebastian Giustinian, recorded on 10 October 1519 that:

. . . his Majesty is twenty-nine years old and extremely handsome; nature could not have done more for him; he is much handsomer than any other sovereign in Christendom, a great deal handsomer than the King of France; very fair, and his whole frame admirably proportioned. . . He is very accomplished; a good musician; composes well; is a most capital horseman; a fine jouster; speaks good French, Latin and Spanish; is very religious, hears three masses daily when he hunts, and sometimes five on other days. . . He is very fond indeed of hunting, and never takes this diversion without tiring eight or ten horses. . . He is extremely fond of tennis, at which game it is the prettiest thing in the world to see him play, his fair skin glowing through a shirt of the finest texture. . . He is affable, gracious, harms no one, does not covet his neighbour's goods, and is satisfied with his own dominions. . .

Yet, in the same despatch, Giustinian also went out of his way to emphasise the power of Henry VIII's chief minister Cardinal Wolsey by 1519:

. . . this cardinal is the person who rules both the king and the entire kingdom. On the ambassador's first arrival in England, he used to say to him, 'His Majesty will do so and so'; subsequently, by degrees, he went forgetting himself, and so commenced saying, 'We shall do so and so'; at this present he has reached such a pitch that he says, 'I shall do so and so'.

Another foreign envoy, the Emperor Charles V's ambassador Eustace Chapuys, was no less impressed, in 1535, by the power of Thomas Cromwell. Following the downfall of Cardinal Wolsey at the end of the 1520s, he reported, Cromwell undertook to make Henry VIII:

> . . . the richest sovereign that ever reigned in England. He promised so fairly that the king at once retained him upon the council . . . Since that time he has risen above everyone, except it be the Lady Anne Boleyn, and the world says he has more credit with his master than ever the cardinal had. The cardinal shared his influence with several others but, now, there is not a person who does anything except Cromwell.

A few years later in 1540, however, the French ambassador Charles de Marillac chose to focus, instead, on the king himself and his scathing verdict is certainly in sharp contrast to those brought in by Venetian envoys Lorenzo Pasqualigo and Sebastian Giustinian early in Henry VIII's reign:

> . . . this prince seems tainted, among other vices, with three which in a king may be called plagues. The first is that he is so covetous that all the riches in the world would not satisfy him. Hence the ruin of the abbeys. . . Hence, too, the accusation of so many rich men who, whether condemned or acquitted, are always plucked. . . Everything is a good prize, and he does not reflect that to make himself rich he has impoverished his people, and does not gain in goods what he loses in renown. . . Thence proceeds the second plague, distrust and fear. This king,

Thomas Wolsey, (1473–1530).
When Henry VIII became King
of England in 1509, Wolsey
became the King's almoner
and by 1514 he had become the
controlling figure in virtually all
matters of state and extremely
powerful within the Church.
The highest political position he
attained was Lord Chancellor.
A painting by Sampson Strong.
Christ Church, Oxford

Stephen Gardiner, (1483–1555).
Gardiner took charge of
negotiations for the annulment
of the marriage of Henry VIII
and Catherine of Aragon
from 1528 to 1529. He was
unsuccessful. Nevertheless
Henry fully appreciated
Gardiner's services and he was
appointed the king's secretary.
A painting by Quinten Massys,
c. 1510. *Liechtenstein Museum*

Sir Henry Guildford, (1489–1532). On the accession of Henry VIII, Henry Guildford was a young man of twenty, and a favourite with the new king. Before long he became master of the revels, master of the horse and comptroller of the royal household. A painting by Hans Holbein the Younger, 1527. *Royal Collection, Windsor Castle*

knowing how many changes he has made, and what tragedies and scandals he has created, would fain keep in favour with everybody, but does not trust a single man and will not cease to dip his hand in blood as long as he doubts his people. . . The third plague, lightness and inconstancy, proceeds partly from the other two and partly from the nature of the nation, and has perverted the rights of religion, marriage, faith and promise.

As for the king's subjects, Marillac added, they:

> . . . take example from the prince, and the ministers seek only to undo each other to gain credit, and under cover of their master's well-being each attends to his own. For all the fine words of which they are full they will act only as necessity and interest compel them.

Clearly, as far as Henry VIII's reputation was concerned, the assertion of royal supremacy over the church in the early 1530s and the religious upheavals that followed were pivotal. In his *Acts and Monuments of the Christian Martyrs* published in 1563, for instance, the Protestant John Foxe harboured no doubts that:

> . . . so long as Queen Anne, Thomas Cromwell, Archbishop Cranmer and such like were about him, and could prevail with him, what organ of Christ's glory did more good in the church than he?. . . Thus, while good counsel was about him and could be heard, the king did much good. Once sinister and wicked counsel under subtle and crafty pretences got its foot in, however, and thrust truth and verity out of the prince's ears, where all good things had gone prosperously forward before, now all revolted backwards again.

Unlike Anne Boleyn and Thomas Cromwell, who both lost their heads on Henry VIII's orders, the religiously much more conservative Stephen Gardiner Bishop of Winchester, despite not infrequently questioning the wisdom of royal policy and behaviour in the 1530s and early 1540s, managed to hang on to his; moreover, when writing to Protector Somerset on 6 June 1547, his verdict on the recently deceased king was nothing if not nostalgic:

> I esteemed him, as he was, a wise prince, and whatsoever he wrote or said for the present, he would after consider the matter as wisely as any man, and neither hurt or inwardly disfavour him that had been bold with him; whereof I serve for a proof, for no man could do me hurt during his life. And when he gave me the bishopric of Winchester, he said he had often squared with me, but he loved me never the worse; and for a token thereof gave me the bishopric.

John Fisher, (1469–1535). Fisher was an English Catholic bishop and theologian. He was a man of learning, associated with the intellectuals and political leaders of his day, and eventually became Chancellor of the University of Cambridge. Fisher was executed by order of Henry VIII for refusing to accept the king as Supreme Head of the Church of England and for upholding the Catholic Church's doctrine of papal primacy.

ANNA BOLLINA ⁓ VXOR HEN VIII.

Anne Boleyn, (*c.* 1501–1536). Anne was the daughter of Thomas Boleyn, 1st Earl of Wiltshire, and his wife, Lady Elizabeth Howard. In 1522 she secured a post at court as maid of honour to Henry VIII's queen, Catherine of Aragon. Early in 1526, Henry VIII began his pursuit of Anne. She resisted his attempts to seduce her, refusing to become his mistress. It soon became the one absorbing object of Henry's desires to annul his marriage to Queen Catherine so he would be free to marry Anne.

There are many portraits based on the common representation of Anne Boleyn as shown here, but recent modern research has questioned the accuracy of her features in these depictions.

Thomas Cromwell, (*c.* 1485–1540). Cromwell was a member Cardinal Thomas Wolsey's, council and by 1529 he was Wolsey's secretary and most senior adviser. By the autumn of 1531 Cromwell had taken control of the supervision of the king's legal and parliamentary affairs, working closely with Thomas Audley, and had joined the inner circle of the Council. Painting by Hans Holbein the Younger, (1532–33).

Perhaps such nostalgia was not misplaced since, when he fell out with Somerset a few weeks later, Gardiner was promptly imprisoned: indeed, he ended up spending much of Edward VI's reign (1547–1553) incarcerated in the Tower of London. Both Foxe and Gardiner penned reasonably sober judgements on Henry VIII. Not so Anthony Gilbey who, writing in Calvinist Geneva in 1558, declared venomously that 'in the time of that tyrant and lecherous monster' there was 'no Reformation' in England but, rather, 'a deformation'. And Ulpian Fulwell, in 1575, was no less extravagant in praising a king who had proved himself 'a treasure' to England, 'a tender father' to his 'faithful and loving subjects', and 'an ornament' to the world.

Historians of Henry VIII and his times are fortunate in being able to draw on the published work of several contemporary and near-contemporary chroniclers, biographers and historians. Prominent among them is the astute and well-informed Italian humanist Polydore Vergil. After several years resident in England, Vergil was commissioned to write his *Anglica Historia* by Henry VII in 1507. His completed narrative, covering England's history from ancient times to 1509 and dedicated to Henry VIII, was published in 1534. Two decades later in 1555, when a new edition was printed, the narrative was extended to include coverage of Henry VIII's reign 1509–1537. A shrewd observer of the early Tudor political scene, Vergil was particularly struck by similarities between Henry VIII and his Yorkist grandfather Edward IV (1461–1483):

> . . . just as Edward was the most warmly thought of by the English people among all English kings, so this successor of his, Henry, was very like him in general appearance, in greatness of mind and generosity, and for that reason was the more acclaimed and approved of by all.

Indeed, declared Vergil, at the start of his reign, 'everybody loved' Henry VIII, not least on account of his:

> . . . handsome bearing, his comely and manly features (in which one could discern as much authority as goodwill), his outstanding physical strength, remarkable memory, aptness at all the arts of both war and peace, skill at arms and on horseback, scholarship of no mean order, thorough knowledge of music, and his humanity, benevolence and self-control.

Vergil was no mere apologist for Henry VIII, however, or his ministers for that matter: for instance, he made no attempt to disguise his loathing for Cardinal Wolsey and, as a man whose loyalty to Rome never seriously wavered, he clearly had deep reservations as well about the king's policies and behaviour during the early 1530s.

Polydore Vergil's consistently hostile treatment of Wolsey no doubt reflected the fact that, for several months in 1515, he was imprisoned on the cardinal's orders. Wolsey's biographer George Cavendish, by

Edward IV, (1442–1483, king 1461–1483); maternal grandfather of Henry VIII. Henry very much took after his grandfather who was temperamentally lazy and given over to the enjoyment of the pleasures of life. Philippe de Commynes described him in his younger days as 'a man so vigorous and handsome that he might have been made for the pleasures of the flesh'. Edward's impressive physique and height (approximately 6 feet 4½ inches) were set off by splendid clothes. *National Portrait Gallery*

Elizabeth Woodville, (*c.* 1437–1492). Elizabeth was Queen consort of Edward IV from 1464 until his death in 1483. Through her daughter, Elizabeth of York, who married Henry VII, she is an ancestor of every English monarch since Henry VIII and every Scottish monarch since James V of Scotland.

ELIZABETHA · VXOR HENRICI · VII ·

Elizabeth of York, (1466–1503). Elizabeth was the daughter of Edward IV and Elizabeth Woodville, and from 1486, Queen consort of Henry VII until her death. Elizabeth of York was a renowned beauty, inheriting her parents' fair hair and complexion. All other Tudor monarchs inherited her reddish gold hair and the trait became synonymous with the dynasty. Elizabeth and Henry VII had seven children: Arthur, Prince of Wales, (1486–1502); Margaret, Queen consort of Scotland, (1489–1541); Henry VIII of England, (1491–1547); Elizabeth, (1492–1495); Mary, Queen consort of France, (1496–1533); Edmund, (1499–1500) and Katherine, (born and died 1503). Elizabeth died of an infection shortly after giving birth to Katherine.

contrast, very much emphasised that 'this cardinal was my lord and master, whom in his life I served, and so remained with him after his fall, continually during the term of all his troubles, until he died'. Not surprisingly, when he eventually penned his *Life and Death of Cardinal Wolsey* in the mid-1550s, his former status very much influenced and informed the resulting portrayal of both the cardinal himself and the second Tudor king whom he served. During his early years on the throne, Cavendish declared emphatically, Henry VIII was:

> . . . young and lusty, disposed all to mirth and pleasure and to
> follow his desire and appetites, nothing minding to labour in
> the busy affairs of this realm. The which the cardinal perceived
> very well and took upon him, therefore, to unburden the king
> of so weighty a charge and troublesome business, putting
> him in comfort that he shall not need to spare any time of his

pleasure for any business that should of necessity happen in the council, as long as he, being there and having the king's authority, doubted not to see all things sufficiently furnished and perfected.

The young Henry VIII, Cavendish further emphasised:

> . . . loved nothing worse than to be forced to do anything contrary to his royal will and pleasure. This the cardinal knew very well, having a secret intelligence of the king's natural inclination, and as fast as other councillors advised the king to leave his pleasures and attend to the affairs of his realm, so busily did the cardinal persuade him to the contrary; which delighted him much and caused him to have the greatest affection and love for the cardinal. Thus the cardinal ruled all them that before ruled him.

Sadly, much of George Cavendish's fascinating near-contemporary biography of Wolsey remained unpublished until the nineteenth century. Edward Hall's massive *Union of the Two Noble and Illustrious Families of Lancaster and York*, by contrast, found its way into print within a few months of its author's death in 1547 and, as a result, has had far more influence then Cavendish (or Polydore Vergil, for that matter) in helping to forge Henry VIII's historical reputation. A Cambridge graduate and lawyer, Hall was very much a man of his time and a great admirer of the Tudor dynasty; he sat in the Reformation Parliament in the early 1530s; and, as a Protestant sympathiser, he strongly supported most of the political and religious measures promulgated there by his royal master. Clearly, when penning his chronicle, Hall revelled in the dramatic potential of the story he was telling while, at the same time, proving himself a careful and thoughtful organiser of the rich material available to him. He obviously enjoyed, in particular, immersing himself in the detail of

LEFT: A page from the first edition of *Actes and Monuments*, also known as *Foxe's Book of Martyrs*, published in 1563. John Foxe (1516–1587), a historian, was the author of *Actes and Monuments*, an account of Christian martyrs throughout Western history but emphasizing the sufferings of English Protestants through to the reign of Queen Mary.

ABOVE: Polydore Vergil of Urbino, (*c.* 1470–1555). Vergil was an Italian humanist scholar, historian, priest and diplomat who spent most of his life in England. Vergil's history of England, the *Anglica Historia*, was begun at the instigation of King Henry VII, probably in 1507. This first version was completed in 1512–13 but the work was not published until 1534.

A monk in despair: a woodcut from Polydore Vergil's *De Inventoribus Rerum*. Vergil's *De Inventoribus Rerum* was published in 1499. It was a history of origins and inventions, including printing, describing in three books the 'first begetters' of all human activities.

An illustration from George Cavendish's manuscript biography of Wolsey. This drawing, presumably the work of George Cavendish, shows the Cardinal with all due pomp. Wolsey is riding in procession preceded by his great crosses, as Archbishop and legate; and his Cardinal's hat. George Cavendish, (1497–*c.* 1562), entered the service of Cardinal Wolsey as gentleman-usher about 1522, and stayed in his service until Wolsey's death in 1530. Part of his manuscript was published in 1641 under the title: *Thomas Wolsey, Late Cardinall, his Lyffe and Deathe* but it was not fully and accurately transcribed and published until 1825.

The Fall of the Cardinal. Another illustration from George Cavendish's manuscript biography of Wolsey, showing the Cardinal's fall from grace. The Cardinal surrenders the great seal of England, symbolising the Lord Chancellorship, to his enemies, the Dukes of Norfolk and Suffolk, October 1529.

what happened in his own lifetime: hence why his final chapter, 'The Triumphant Reign of Henry VIII', occupies almost half the pages of a narrative commencing in 1399. Even Hall's critics, moreover, recognise his chronicle as a source of prime importance for the second Tudor's reign, not least because its author was an active participant in some events and a conscientious eye-witness observer of others. Typical, perhaps, is this description of Henry VIII at the time of his coronation in 1509:

> The features of his body, his goodly personage, his amiable visage and his princely countenance, together with the noble qualities of his royal estate, are known to every man; however, for lack of cunning, I cannot express the gifts of Grace and of nature with which God has endowed him.

As for his clothing, Hall continued:

> . . . his Grace wore a robe of crimson velvet, furred with ermine, a jacket or coat of raised gold, and a placard embroidered with diamonds, rubies, emeralds, great pearls and other rich stones; the knights and esquires of his body were in crimson velvet; and all his gentlemen, officers and household servants were apparelled in scarlet.

During a royal progress in 1511, Hall further noted, the king indulged 'in shooting, singing, dancing, wrestling, casting the bar, playing at the recorders, flutes and virginals, and in setting of songs and making of ballads, as well as setting two godly masses'. By the time he met Francis I of France at the Field of the Cloth of Gold in 1520 dressed 'in a garment of cloth of silver as thick as might be' and 'marvellous to behold', moreover, Henry had become 'the most goodliest prince that ever ruled over the realm of England'. As for the meeting itself, Hall records:

. . . the two Kings met and embraced each other in sight of both
the nations and on horseback; then the two kings alighted and
embraced again with benign and courteous manner each to the
other, with sweet and goodly words of greeting; and, after a few
words, these two noble kings went together arm in arm into the
rich tent of cloth of gold, there set on the ground for such purpose.

Over a decade later in 1532, when controversy over the validity of
Henry VIII's marriage to Catherine of Aragon was at its height, Hall
may well he drawing on first-hand knowledge in reporting the king's
declaration to Thomas Audley, Speaker of the House of Commons,
that:

. . . he wished his marriage had been valid, for then he would
never have been troubled in his conscience; but the doctors of
the universities, said he, have determined the marriage to be
void, and detestable before God, which conscientious doubts
caused him to abstain from her company, and not foolish or
wanton appetite. 'For I am', said he, '41 years old, at which age a
man's lust is not so quick as in lusty youth'.

Hall's narrative post-1533, although probably not put together in its
final form until after the chronicler's death, nevertheless seems to
be firmly based on archival material bequeathed by him. And this
passage, recording Henry VIII's triumphant entry into Boulogne
after the town fell into English hands in 1544, certainly has a ring of
authority about it:

The king's highness, with a naked sword borne before him by
the lord marquis of Dorset, rode into Boulogne like a noble
and valiant conqueror, and the trumpeters standing on the
walls of the town sounded their trumpets at his entry, to the
great comfort of all the king's true subjects who beheld it. . .

Henry VIII at the Field of the Cloth of Gold. The site was at Balinghem between Ardres in France and Guînes in the then English held Pale of Calais. The meeting was arranged to increase the bond of friendship between Francis I of France (1494–1547, king from 1515 to 1547) and Henry VIII of England (1491–1547, king from 1509 to 1547) following the Anglo-French treaty of 1514. The meeting lasted some seventeen days, from 7 to 24 June 1520.

When the king had set all things there in such order as to his wisdom seemed best, he returned to England to the great rejoicing of all his subjects.

Very much in the tradition of Edward Hall, and drawing heavily on his work, was the Elizabethan chronicle traditionally attributed to Raphael Holinshed and first published in 1578. In fact it seems to have been compiled by a syndicate of writers and its tendency to plagiarise Hall is never more apparent than in Holinshed's account of Henry VIII's meeting with Francis I in 1520:

The two kings met, accompanied by such a number of the nobility of both realms, so richly appointed in apparel and costly jewels, that it was a wonder to behold and view them. . . Meeting in the field they saluted each other in most loving wise, first on horseback, and, after alighting on foot, embraced with courteous words, to the great rejoicing of the beholders. And after they had thus saluted each other, they went together into a rich tent of cloth of gold, there set up for the purpose, in which they passed the time in pleasant talk.

Original Designs to Magnify Henry's Glory. Each king tried to outdo the other with dazzling tents and clothes, grand feasts, music, jousting and games. This drawing is thought to be an original design for the tents, connected by a series of galleries. *British Library*

2

Seventeenth, Eighteenth and Nineteenth Century Judgements

P ERHAPS THE GREATEST CLAIM TO fame of the so-called *Chronicle of Raphael Holinshed* is that it eventually provided the prime source for William Shakespeare's Plantagenet history plays. The same also goes for *Henry VIII*, probably written in 1613 and another play traditionally attributed to Shakespeare: indeed, it drew on Holinshed more than any of the earlier plays, for plot, characterisation, even the wording of dialogue. No wonder there has long been a question mark over whether Shakespeare wrote the play at all. Literary scholars have certainly argued about this for years, and continue to do so, but most now seem to agree that the final text probably resulted from a collaboration between Shakespeare, virtually at the end of his career, and a rising young playwright John Fletcher. It is certainly a very odd play. Whereas Shakespeare's *Richard III*, for instance, very much focuses on the king himself and the tyrannical nature of his rule, *Henry VIII* most emphatically does not revolve around the second Tudor's personality and behaviour; only two of his wives (Catherine of Aragon and Anne Boleyn) figure in the text; and the play touches but lightly on the English Reformation. Chronologically, it covers just thirteen of the thirty-eight years Henry VIII was on the throne, from the Field of the Cloth of Gold in 1520 to the birth of the future queen Elizabeth I in 1533; the king himself is absent from many scenes; and, when he does appear, he seems to bear but scant resemblance to the historical Henry: rather, we are presented with what amounts to a romantic and idealised portrait of a semi-divine monarch anxious, above all, to facilitate the triumph of good over evil. Far more memorable, anyway, are scenes highlighting 'this top-proud fellow', 'this holy fox', 'this bold bad man' Cardinal Wolsey, in a plot that seems to progress inexorably to the birth of Henry VIII's daughter Elizabeth in 1533:

> This royal infant—heaven still move about her!—
> Though in her cradle, yet now promises
> Upon this land a thousand thousand blessings,
> Which time shall bring to ripeness. She shall be—
> But few now living can behold that goodness—
> A pattern to all princes living with her,
> And all that shall succeed. . .
> She shall be, to the happiness of England,
> An aged princess; many days shall see her
> And yet no day without a deed to crown it.

Clearly, the Henry VIII of Shakespeare and Fletcher's early seventeenth-century play bears little resemblance to the historical king, maybe because it was specifically commissioned for performance during celebrations of the wedding of James I's daughter Elizabeth in 1613. Sir Walter Raleigh's very different portrayal of the second Tudor, in his *History of the World* published in 1614, may also be a product of circumstance since, at the time, its author was a royal prisoner in the Tower of London:

> . . . how many servants did he advance in haste and, with the change of his fancy, ruin again, no man knowing for what offence? How many wives did he cut off, and cast off, as his

fancy and affection changed? How many princes of the blood did he execute? Even on his death bed, when on the point of having to account to God for the abundance of blood already spilt, he imprisoned the Duke of Norfolk the father and executed the Earl of Surrey the son.

 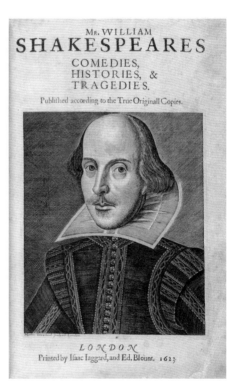

LEFT: Raphael Holinshed's Chronicle. The title page from volume 3, 1586 edition. Shakespeare drew on Holinshed for both his Plantagenet history plays and Henry VIII.

RIGHT: William Shakespeare, (1564–1616). Sometime between 1585 and 1592, Shakespeare began a successful career in London as an actor, writer, and part-owner of a playing company called the Lord Chamberlain's Men, later known as the King's Men. He appears to have retired to Stratford around 1613, at age 49, where he died three years later. Shakespeare produced most of his known work between 1589 and 1613.

In the century following Henry VIII's death, Raleigh was not alone in criticising the king's personal conduct; moreover, since he was generally held responsible for all policies pursued during his reign, any blame for their evil consequences tended to be heaped on him as well. Not until 1649 did Lord Herbert of Cherbury publish his *Life and Reign of King Henry the Eighth* and, as the king's first biographer, he was also significantly more scholarly than most earlier commentators. In particular, he attempted to draw a firm distinction between the private character of Henry VIII the man and the public acts of Henry VIII the king, and firmly believed that, despite all his crimes, 'he was one of the most glorious princes of his time'. As for his critics, it was 'discontented clergymen (for his relinquishing of the pope's authority and overthrowing the monasteries) or affronted women (for diverse examples against their own sex) that first opposed and cried him down'.

In 1679 Gilbert Burnet Bishop of Salisbury, determined to counter what he saw as alarming signs of resurgent Roman Catholicism in Charles II's reign and convinced of the need to 'compose our differences at home, establish a closer correspondence with reformed churches abroad and secure us from the restless and wicked practices of the Church of Rome', published the first volume of his influential *History of the Reformation in England* (covering the reign of Henry VIII). Although much criticised both in his own time and since, Burnet was both shrewd and conscious of the need to tell an accurate story; moreover, he was perfectly willing to criticise not only Henry VIII's treatment of his wives but even his execution of Roman Catholic stalwarts such as Bishop John Fisher of Rochester and Sir Thomas More. Nevertheless, as a staunch defender of the later seventeenth-century Anglican church, he was also convinced that, 'if we consider the great things that were done' by Henry VIII, 'we must acknowledge that there was a signal providence of God in raising up a king of his temper, for clearing the way to that blessed work which followed'. As for Henry's historical reputation, he ought to be

Sir Walter Raleigh, (*c.* 1554–1618). Raleigh rose rapidly in the favour of Queen Elizabeth and was knighted in 1585. Instrumental in the English colonisation of North America, Raleigh was granted a royal patent to explore Virginia, which paved the way for future English settlements. Raleigh was eventually imprisoned in the Tower by James I and, while there, he wrote many treatises and the first volume of *The Historie of the World* (first edition published 1614). Portrait of Sir Walter Raleigh, 1588. *National Portrait Gallery*

reckoned 'among the great rather than the good princes' who have ruled England:

> He exercised so much severity on men of both Catholic and Protestant persuasions that writers on both sides have laid open his faults and taxed his cruelty. But, as neither of them were much obliged to him, so none have taken so much care to set forth his good qualities as his enemies have done to enlarge on his vices.

The philosopher-cum-historian David Hume in 1759 was certainly no great admirer of Henry VIII, the authoritarian regime he established or, for that matter, the English Reformation. He was genuinely puzzled, however, that:

> . . . notwithstanding his cruelty, his extortion, his violence, his arbitrary administration, this prince not only acquired the regard of his subjects, but never was the object of their hatred.

Gilbert Burnet, (1643–1715). A Scottish philosopher and historian, and Bishop of Salisbury, Gilbert Burnet was respected as a preacher, and an academic, as well as a writer. A portrait after John Riley, c. 1689–1691.

The only explanation, Hume concluded rather desperately, must be that the English:

> . . . in that age were so thoroughly subdued that, like eastern slaves, they were inclined to admire those acts of violence and tyranny which were exercised over themselves, and at their own expense.

Henry Hallam, in his *Constitutional History of England from the Accession of Henry VII to the Death of George II* (published in 1827) believed that Henry VIII, despite the 'language of eulogy' embraced by some commentators after his demise, never really 'conciliated his people's affection'; rather, the 'perfect fear which attended him must have cast out love'. Nevertheless, Hallam continued, the king did have 'a few qualities that deserve esteem and several which a nation is pleased to behold in a sovereign'; his 'manners were affable and his temper generous'; and 'our forefathers cherished the

LEFT: David Hume, (1711–1776). Hume was an eminent Scottish philosopher and historian. In this portrait by his friend Allan Ramsay, 1763, he is resting his left arm informally on two books possibly alluding to his own publications such as his *Treatise on Human Nature* and *The History of England. National Galleries Scotland*

RIGHT: Henry Hallam, (1777–1859). Educated at Eton and Christ Church, Oxford, Hallam practised as a barrister on the Oxford circuit for some years before turning to history. *The Constitutional History of England* was published in 1827. A portrait by Thomas Phillips, held at Clevedon Court, Somerset.

king's memory', in particular, for his share in the Reformation as 'the avenging minister of heaven by whose giant arm the chain of superstition was broken and the prison gates cast asunder'. Clearly, in the decades that followed, Victorians became increasingly inclined to regard Henry VIII as an enigmatic and contradictory figure at best, a veritable bogeyman at worst; for many Anglicans it was obviously a matter of great discomfort that the second Tudor, of all men, had a virtually unassailable claim to be regarded as the founder of their church; and, more straightforwardly, Roman Catholics continued to castigate the king as the great apostate, the man who betrayed their church and destroyed its authority in England merely to further his own sordid political and dynastic ends. Most bizarrely of all, in 1884, the Cambridge historian Mandell Creighton even felt exasperated enough to exclaim:

> As for the Tudors, they are awful! I really do not think anyone ought to read the history of the sixteenth century.

Among Victorian historians of Henry VIII and his times, pride of place must surely go to James Anthony Froude, who commenced writing his multi-volume *History of England from the Fall of Cardinal Wolsey to the Defeat of the Spanish Armada* in 1854. Like Henry's first biographer Lord Herbert of Cherbury in 1649, he sought to separate the king's private life from his public behaviour. Henry VIII's 'personal faults were great', he admitted, but:

Mandell Creighton, (1843–1901). Creighton was a Cambridge professor and a bishop of the Church of England rising to become Bishop of London. Creighton's historical work received mixed reviews. He was praised for scrupulous even-handedness, but criticised for not taking a stand against historical excesses. Creighton as Bishop of London, by Sir Hubert von Herkomer. *National Portrait Gallery*

James Anthony Froude, (1818–1894). Froude was a fellow of Exeter College, Oxford, and destined for the Church, but his leanings towards the Oxford Movement raised a storm of controversy and he was forced to resign his fellowship. He took refuge from the popular outcry by residing with his friend Charles Kingsley at Ilfracombe. He completed his *History of England* in 1870. In 1892 Froude was appointed as Regius Professor of Modern History at Oxford.

... far deeper blemishes would be but scars upon the features of a sovereign who in trying times sustained nobly the honour of the English name, and carried the commonwealth securely through the hardest crisis in its history.

As a young man his beauty, physical strength, intelligence and learning were only too evident: indeed, he clearly displayed just those 'splendid tastes in which the English people most delighted'. Unfortunately, his Plantagenet blood and upbringing as a Renaissance prince also endowed him with 'a most intense and imperious will' and 'later in life, when his character was formed, he was forced into collision with difficulties he was ill-equipped to handle'. Even so, he 'displayed natural powers of the highest order'; as a ruler he was 'eminently popular'; and 'if he had died before the divorce was mooted' in 1527, he 'would have been considered by posterity as formed by Providence for the conduct of the Reformation, and his loss would have been deplored as a perpetual calamity'. Although not a wholly committed Protestant himself, moreover, Froude, like Gilbert Burnet before him in 1679, was determined to defend the integrity of the Anglican church and, obviously, this was contentious in itself. Even more so was his portrayal of Henry VIII as a ruler of enormous potential sadly defeated, in the end, by circumstances largely beyond his control. Indeed, Froude soon came under sustained attack from his own contemporaries, even historians of the calibre of J. R. Green and William Stubbs, notwithstanding his avowed and admirable commitment to the study of original sources. 'Those who have examined the printed State Papers' of Henry VIII's reign, he once judiciously mused, 'may form some impression of his industry from the documents which are his own composition and the letters he wrote and received'; however, he continued enthusiastically:

> . . . only persons who have seen the original manuscripts, who have observed the traces of his pen in side-notes and corrections, and the handwritings of his secretaries in diplomatic commissions, drafts of acts of Parliament, in expositions and formularies, in articles of faith, in proclamations, in the countless multitude of documents of all sorts, secular or ecclesiastical, which contain the real history of this extraordinary reign, only they can realise the extent of labour to which he sacrificed himself, and which brought his life to a premature close.

When, years later, the king's biographer A. F. Pollard found 'inadequate justification for the systematic destruction of Froude's *History* which has become the fashion', he was absolutely right.

No Victorian historian enjoyed a wider readership than John Richard Green; indeed, within a year of its publication in 1874, his *Short History of the English People* went through five impressions. Henry VIII, he noted fluently:

John Richard Green, (1837–1883). Green was the son of a tradesman in Oxford. He was educated at Magdalen College School, and then at Jesus College where he is commemorated by the J. R. Green Society. He entered the Church, and served various cures in London. Always an enthusiastic student of history, the little leisure time he had was devoted to research. His book *A Short History of the English People*, appeared in 1874. He later expanded his *Short History* into *A History of the English People* in 4 volumes. (1878–80).

William Stubbs, (1825–1901). Stubbs was educated at Christ Church, Oxford and was elected a fellow of Trinity College, and held the college living of Navestock, Essex, from 1850 to 1866. In 1866, he was appointed Regius Professor of Modern History at Oxford, and held the chair until 1884. On 25 April 1884 he was consecrated Bishop of Chester, and in 1889 became Bishop of Oxford. Both in England and America Bishop Stubbs was universally acknowledged as the head of all English historical scholars, and no English historian of his time was held in equal honour in European countries. He is most widely known for his *Constitutional History of England* (3 vols., 1874–78).

. . . had hardly completed his eighteenth year when he mounted
the throne, but the beauty of his person, his vigour and skill
in arms, seemed matched by a frank and generous temper
and a nobleness of political aims. . . No accession ever excited
greater expectations among a people than that of Henry VIII. . .
Already in stature and strength a king among his fellows, taller
than any, bigger than any, a mighty wrestler, a mighty hunter,
an archer of the best, a knight who bore down rider after rider
in the tourney, the young monarch combined with his bodily
lordliness a largeness and versatility of mind.

When he raised his 'low-born favourite' Thomas Wolsey to be 'head
of church and state', moreover, the king was at the same time:

. . . gathering all religious as well as all civil authority into his
personal grasp. The nation which trembled before Wolsey
learned to tremble before the king who could destroy Wolsey
by a breath. . . The ten years which follow the fall of Wolsey are
among the most momentous in our history. . . The one great
institution which could still offer resistance to the royal will
was struck down. The church became a mere instrument of
the central despotism. The people learned their helplessness in
rebellions easily suppressed and avenged with ruthless severity.
A reign of terror, organised with consummate and merciless
skill, held England panic-stricken at Henry's feet . . . and, by
1540, the monarchy had reached the height of its power.

And, for Green at least, the last years of Henry VIII's reign (1540–
1547) seem to have been no more than an anti-climax since he
dismissed them in a mere page and a half!

William Stubbs, Oxford University's professor of modern history
from 1866 to 1884 when he left to become bishop of Chester, was
as distinguished a professional historian as any the Victorian age

produced. Now best remembered for a magisterial three-volume survey of medieval English constitutional history, he did also publish, in 1881, a couple of interesting lectures on Henry VIII and his reign. He was certainly determined to distance himself from received wisdom: 'I do not believe the king to have been the monster of lust and blood' portrayed by so many Roman Catholic writers, he declared, but 'nor can I accept at all the picture Mr Froude has drawn'. Stubbs' own Henry VIII was 'every inch a king' both physically and mentally; he was 'no more vicious than many kings who have maintained a very fair reputation in history'; and, as for 'the greatest and most critical changes of his reign,' he himself was their 'main originator'. The king, in fact, was:

> . . . neither the puppet of parties, nor the victim of circumstances, nor the shifty politician, nor the capricious tyrant, but a man of light and leading, of power, force and foresight, a man of opportunities, stratagems and surprises, but no less of iron will and determined purpose. . . The unhappy, most unhappy history of his wives, has brought upon him an amount of moral hatred which is excessive, but he was cruelly, royally vindictive; there was in him an ever-increasing, ever-encroaching self-will, ever grasping and grasping more and more of power: a self-will guided by a high intellect, and that sort of sincerity which arises from a thorough belief in himself.

'I am not prepared to deny that deep, cunning, unscrupulous men, like Thomas Cromwell, traded on their knowledge of the king's character', Stubbs added; however, 'not one of those who tried to work their own ends through Henry escaped the doom to which false friends and open foes alike found their way'. As for Stubbs' conclusion, it was nothing if not enigmatic:

Have I drawn the outline of a monster? Well, perhaps; but not the popular notion of this particular portent. A strong, high-spirited, ruthless, disappointed, solitary creature; a thing to hate, or to pity, or to smile at, or to shudder at, or to wonder at, but not to judge.

A Rediscovered Mural of Henry VIII. This is said to be the only surviving example of a wall painting of Henry VIII, even if not a flattering depiction. It was found by a couple in Milverton, Somerset, after they had removed layers of old wood panels, plaster and wallpaper from their living room wall to prepare for redecoration. The artist is unknown, but the property once belonged to Stephen Gardiner who was Archdeacon of Taunton at the time that the mural was painted (*c.* 1529).

3

Modern Verdicts

T HE CLASSIC MODERN INTERPRETATION OF Henry VIII, and a notably sympathetic one, is that of A. F. Pollard in a biography of the king first published in 1902. Although he made little use of archives, moreover, Pollard's knowledge of the detailed content of recently published volumes of *Letters and Papers, Foreign and Domestic, of the Reign of Henry VIII* was exhaustive. Clearly, too, his portrayal of both the king and his behaviour also owed a great deal to previous analyses and verdicts, notably those of J. A. Froude and J. R. Green. As a young man Pollard's own Henry VIII was both athletic and intellectual, and a very regal figure, but not much interested in the detailed business of government, preferring to leave that largely to others while giving himself over to the pursuit of princely pleasures. Hence why, between 1514 and 1529, he happily delegated so much day-to-day authority to Cardinal Wolsey. When Wolsey failed to get him a divorce from Catherine of Aragon, however, the cardinal was peremptorily dismissed; Henry now took the reins of power firmly into his own hands; and, from 1530 until his death in 1547, the king himself ruled. During that time, moreover, the power of both monarchy and nation were significantly advanced. Pollard's mature Henry VIII was certainly egotistical, self-willed and all too easily tempted down the road to despotism and tyranny; yet, and here we see the king's early twentieth-century biographer in full rhetorical flow, he also possessed:

> . . . the strength of a lion and, like a lion, he used it. . . Without him the storm of the Reformation would still have burst over England but, without him, it might also have been far more terrible. Every drop of blood shed under Henry VIII might have been a river under a feebler king. Instead of a stray execution here and there, conducted always with a scrupulous regard for legal forms, wars of religion might have desolated the land and swept away thousands of lives.

As for Pollard's final verdict on the second Tudor and his reign, it could hardly have been more up-beat:

> Surrounded by faint hearts and fearful minds, Henry VIII neither faltered nor failed. He ruled in a ruthless age with a ruthless hand, he dealt with a violent crisis by methods of blood and iron, and his measures were crowned with whatever sanction worldly success can give. He is Machiavelli's *Prince* in action. . . The spiritual welfare of England entered into his thoughts, if at all, as a minor consideration; but, for her peace and material comfort it was well that she had as her king, in her hour of need, a man, and a man who counted the cost, who faced the risk, and who did with his might whatsoever his hand found to do.

A. F. Pollard's splendidly well-informed and, for the most part, well-rounded 1902 biography of Henry VIII held its own for over half a century, underpinning virtually all textbook accounts of the second Tudor's reign until the 1950s, and not losing its status as standard life of the king until J. J. Scarisbrick's *Henry VIII* was published in 1968.

Not untypical in its interpretation, albeit more readable and more entertaining than most ostensibly scholarly surveys, was Christopher Morris's treatment of Henry VIII and his times in *The Tudors*, first published in 1955 and reprinted several times in the 1960s and 1970s. Handsome, dashing, affable, athletic, musical and linguistically gifted, Morris's charming, self-confident and forceful ruler managed, for many years, to play the role of ideal early sixteenth-century king, even Renaissance 'magnifico'. Yet flaws were always evident as well. Even as a young man he was too often self-indulgent and self-willed; his talents were both ill-disciplined and ill-directed; and, by his later years, he had also become more and more of a tyrant. As for the king's reign, A. F. Pollard's continuing influence is all too apparent in Morris's interpretation. Henry VIII, he declared:

Albert Frederick Pollard, (1869–1948). Pollard was educated at Jesus College, Oxford where he achieved a first class honours degree in Modern History in 1891. He became Assistant Editor of and a contributor to the *Dictionary of National Biography* in 1893. He was Professor of Constitutional History at University College London from 1903 to 1931. He was a member of the Royal Commission on Historical Manuscripts, and founder of the Historical Association, 1906. He was editor of *History*, 1916–1922, and of the *Bulletin of the Institute of Historical Research*, 1923–1939.

. . . contrived to create in the minds of his subjects a new interpretation of the state and to touch their imaginations in a way that no English king had done before. He embodied and personified in their eyes that self-contained, self-sufficing, sovereign *imperium* for the sake of which he shed innocent blood, broke the clergy, shattered the unity of Christendom and defied with impunity all the powers of Europe.

Religious and social revolution, moreover, was:

. . . almost certain to overtake the England which Henry VIII inherited but he saw to it that the revolution was got under government control. By doing so he minimised the inevitable civil strife and bloodshed. And he contrived that the revolution should make and not unmake his sovereign state.

In 1955, the same year as Christopher Morris's *The Tudors* appeared, the Cambridge historian G. R.(later Sir Geoffrey) Elton

John Joseph Scarisbrick, (b. 1928). Professor John Joseph Scarisbrick MBE FRHistS was born in 1928 in London. He is a Tudor historian who taught at Warwick University and the founder of British pro-life charity, LIFE. Scarisbrick was educated at The John Fisher School and later Christ's College, Cambridge, after spending two years in the Royal Air Force. His most critically acclaimed work is *Henry VIII*, published in 1968.

Rowan Atkinson, as Edmund Blackadder, in the *Blackadder* television series set in Tudor England. Ben Elton, nephew of Sir Geoffrey Rudolph Elton, (1921–1994), jointly penned the scripts for this series with Richard Curtis. His uncle was a German-born political and constitutional historian of Britain. He taught at Clare College, Cambridge and was the Regius Professor of Modern History there from 1983 to 1988. Elton was born in Tübingen, Germany, as Gottfried Rudolf Ehrenberg. His parents were the Jewish scholars Victor Ehrenberg and Eva Dorothea Sommer. During the war he worked for the British Army in the intelligence corps and also anglicised his name to Geoffrey Rudolph Elton. In his academic career he elaborated his ideas on Thomas Cromwell and his influence on Henry VIII in his 1955 work, *England under the Tudors*. Surprisingly there are no good reproducible photographs of G. R. Elton: hence the substitution of his nephew's Tudor hero!

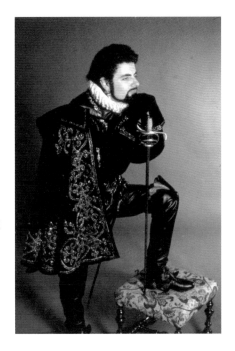

published *England under the Tudors*, perhaps the most widely read and influential of all twentieth-century textbooks covering kingship, politics and government in Tudor England; in 1962, courtesy of the Historical Association, came a typically provocative pamphlet *Henry VIII: An Essay in Revision*; and Elton's mature verdict on the second Tudor king can be found in his 1977 *Reform and Reformation: England 1509–1558*. By then, moreover, his taste for historical controversy had become almost legendary; as for his scholarly reputation, it was now probably as formidable as that of any later twentieth-century historian.

G. R. Elton probably knew the narrative sources for Henry VIII's life and reign as well as any historian ever has and his judgements are certainly not to be sniffed at: Polydore Vergil, for instance, may have demonstrated 'a degree of independence' in his historical narrative but he 'brought a second-rate mind to his systemisation of the past and showed little objectivity in his treatment of his own time'; Edward Hall, by contrast, was not only 'a careful reporter by instinct' but also bequeathed a chronicle 'greatly superior to Polydore's' for the years through which he lived. Nevertheless, for his own interpretation of both Henry VIII himself and the king's role in politics and government, Elton drew mainly on public and private records, letters and, in particular, the papers of Thomas Cromwell, confiscated at the time of his fall in 1540 and fortuitously preserved as a result. The Henry VIII who emerged was neither a political genius nor a Tudor hero. At no time, in Elton's view, was the king an active administrator: he disliked the hard work of government not just in the first half of his reign but throughout it. Consequently, he relied heavily on ministers, notably Thomas Wolsey between 1513 and 1529 and Thomas Cromwell from 1531 to 1540; moreover, Elton believed, the evidence is strong that while a minister held power it was he, not the king, who devised and controlled policy: Henry, more often than not, accepted and endorsed policies he did not initiate. A. F. Pollard, declared Elton, was quite wrong to see a unity in the period 1529 to 1547; rather, there is a great contrast between the largely successful policies of the 1530s (when the king had a highly able minister in Thomas Cromwell) and the 1540s (when he lacked any such minister). Thanks to Cromwell, in fact, the 1530s stand out as a great constructive, even revolutionary, era (as J. R. Green, interestingly enough, had first suggested way back in the 1870s), while the last years of the reign, bedevilled by war and economic crisis, saw Henry both following reckless and unsuccessful policies abroad and failing to cope effectively with mounting religious disunity at home. Personal monarchy under Henry VIII did not mean close attention to business on the king's part as it had under his father Henry VII; rather, it meant putting his personal force behind policies often not of his own devising. 'Henry's greatness', Elton concluded in his 1962 pamphlet:

> . . . lay in the rapid and accurate interpretation of the immediate
> situation, in a dauntless will, and in his choice of advisers; but
> not in originality; and it is doubtful if he was the architect of
> anything, least of all the English Reformation.

The king was intelligent, even intellectual, a good judge of ministers, always willing to pick up ideas from those around him and capable of delegating power. He was no great statesman, admittedly, but nor was he 'the bloated, capricious tyrant of popular mythology'.

Sir Geoffrey Elton's verdict on Henry VIII and the politics of his reign, although massively influential, never hardened into a new orthodoxy; on the contrary, it soon began to be subjected to considerable criticism especially Elton's interpretation of the 1530s and the role of Thomas Cromwell. Even Elton himself, over the years, modified his views a bit, most notably in respect of political faction and its importance. Yet he never budged significantly from his 1962 verdict on Henry VIII personally while, for him at least, Cromwell's role in the 1530s, whether as the presiding genius who made possible the establishment of royal supremacy in the church, the master of administrative procedures who inaugurated a veritable revolution in government, or even the shrewd and ruthless manipulator of courtly politics for years on end, always remained absolutely pivotal.

Very different in interpretation was the biography of Henry VIII by J. J. Scarisbrick, Elton's former student, published in 1968, not least in its cautious return to A. F. Pollard's contention that the king himself must take responsibility for the devising and guiding of policy from at least 1529: in particular, Henry VIII rather than Thomas Cromwell once more became the driving force behind the English Reformation. Throughout, indeed, the framework of Scarisbrick's unfolding narrative owed more to Pollard than to Elton: here, once more, we have the inexperienced and pleasure-loving young king of the early years; the dominant figure of Cardinal Wolsey for a decade and a half; the gradual assertion of Henry VIII's personal control of politics and government from about 1528; the steady progress towards establishing royal supremacy in the church in the 1530s; and, in the king's last years, the employment of newly found power and wealth to revive traditional English ambitions in Scotland and France. As for the king himself, he was a 'formidable and captivating man who wore regality with splendid conviction', a 'prodigy, a sun-king, a *stupor mundi*, who raised the monarchy to near-idolatry'; for some of his subjects at least, he was 'everything that a people could wish him to be, a bluff confident patriot king who was master of his realm and who feared no one'; and, 'by the end of his long reign, despite everything, he was undisputedly revered, indeed, in some strange way, loved'. Even so, Scarisbrick concluded:

> . . . it is difficult to think of any truly generous or selfless action performed by him. . . His French wars brought him little more than 'ungracious dogholes' and ephemeral international prestige. . . He struck down incomparable men and women like Catherine of Aragon, Sir Thomas More and Thomas Cromwell. . . Maybe Henry was no more unaware and irresponsible than many kings have been; but rarely, if ever, have the unawareness and irresponsibility of a king proved more costly of material benefit to his people.

Inevitably, G. R. Elton soon responded to Scarisbrick's biography but, interestingly enough, his reactions were largely positive. While retaining much of A. F. Pollard's outline, he emphasised, this was 'more learned, more accurate and a better book'. The Henry VIII who emerges from its pages is great and formidable, a man of plans and purposes, but also frivolous and whimsical, eclectic in both ideas and action, and fundamentally not very competent; moreover, there is much less indication here of the king's much vaunted understanding of his time and people than there is evidence of his heedless wilfulness and rash selfishness. This king, Elton concluded, is clearly 'a badly flawed hero', even if he remains 'a hero nonetheless'.

Although, even after four decades, J. J. Scarisbrick's *Henry VIII* still remains the best single-volume scholarly biography of the second Tudor, a truly awesome amount has been written since 1968 about both the king himself and his thirty-eight year reign. In 1984, for instance, Jasper Ridley published a new popular biography of the king, noting, in particular, that many of those who knew Henry VIII, among them Cardinal Wolsey, Sir Thomas More and Archbishop Cranmer, very much agreed about this 'lion who, knowing his strength, cannot be ruled' and this:

> . . . prince of a royal courage who cannot be persuaded from his will and appetite, and who will not be bridled nor be against-said in any of his requests; who reacts to every concession and sign of weakness by pressing home his advantage and demanding more, but when confronted by firmness and resistance, becomes affable and retreats.

Although 'always the tall, jovial *bon vivant*, with his zest for life, his love of music and the company of ladies, and his cruel, piggy eyes', moreover, no statesman has ever been more aware than Henry VIII that 'politics is the art of the possible'. And above all, for Ridley, he was very much:

> . . . a product of his time. Only an early sixteenth-century king could have behaved in the way he did. We can imagine Wolsey or Thomas Cromwell living as efficient administrators in other centuries, but it is impossible to imagine Henry VIII as anything except an absolute hereditary sixteenth-century monarch. His regime was in many ways remarkably similar to the totalitarian regimes of the twentieth century.

Prominent among academic historians of Tudor England since the later 1970s has been John Guy, another former student of G. R. Elton, who, in 1988, found Henry VIII's character 'fascinating, threatening and sometimes morbid'; as for the king's 'egoism, self-righteousness and capacity to brood', they 'sprang from the fusion of an able but second-rate mind with what looks suspiciously like an inferiority complex'. When it came to the formulation of policy, Guy believed, this Henry was so eager to conquer and 'emulate the glorious victories of the Black Prince and Henry V' in France that, over and over again, 'the efforts of his more constructive councillors were bedevilled, and overthrown, by his chivalric dreams, and by costly wars, that wasted men, money and equipment: his reign, in fact, saw 'the boldest and most offensive invasions of France' since the early fifteenth century. John Guy had no doubt, either, that Henry VIII wielded 'decisive influence' on topics ranging from foreign diplomacy and the tactics of his first divorce to the definition of royal supremacy and the theology of the church of England in the 1540s. Since the king himself, not Wolsey or Cromwell, was always ultimately in charge, moreover, ministers who pursued policies not approved by him always did so at their own peril; he added 'imperial' concepts of kingship to existing 'feudal' ones; and, eventually, he 'sought to give the words *rex imperator* a meaning unseen since the days of the Roman Empire'.

Even more positive, in 2002, were the conclusions of Cambridge historian Richard Rex. Of all English kings, he declared dramatically, 'Henry VIII has left the deepest impression on the imagination of posterity': here, indeed, was a man 'who could dominate the council table or even, on occasion, the Houses of Parliament', a man 'to whom it was difficult to say no', a man who 'would overthrow a church to obtain a divorce', and a man 'willing to sacrifice ministers and friends, even wives and children, on the altar of dynastic interest'. As for the second Tudor's legacy, Rex was even more outspoken:

For good or ill, intentionally or not, Henry VIII's reign proved a
turning point in English history. To his reign can be traced the
roots of the Church of England, the seeds of the Irish Question,
the birth of the English Bible, the founding of the Privy
Council, and the principle of the omnicompetence of statute.
His reign saw the destruction of English monasticism, which
had helped shape the society and landscape of England for
nearly a millennium. As a result, it also witnessed the greatest
shift in landholding since the Norman Conquest, and saw the
landed wealth of the Crown reach its highest ever level. His
reign, in short, saw something little less than a revolution.

Over the last quarter of a century no historian of Henry VIII and
his times has made a greater impact than David Starkey. Yet another
former student of Sir Geoffrey Elton, he first systematically set out
his stall on early sixteenth-century personalities, politics and power
in an immensely readable 1985 study of *The Reign of Henry VIII*.
Despite an already emerging reputation for expressing controversial
opinions and putting forward contentious interpretations, moreover,
Starkey did concur in several elements of traditional portrayals of
the second Tudor king. Henry VIII, he emphasised, was tall and
well-built as a young man, only becoming massively fat in his later
years; he was intelligent, with a good memory and a nice eye for
detail; he was a shrewd judge of men and had an undoubted flair for
both self-projection and propaganda. His theological knowledge was
considerable and he had a real interest, too, in things mechanical.
Nor did Starkey demur from the familiar picture of young Henry
as a great sportsman and athlete: indeed, he argued, such was
the king's addiction to sport, so often admired by contemporary
commentators, that it seriously interfered with any systematic royal
application to the business of government. Jousting, tennis, hunting,
hawking: these were the dominant interests of Henry VIII in his
early years as king and, not surprisingly, he surrounded himself

with convivial young men who shared his enthusiasms. From the start, too, he began to display character traits which did not augur well for the future. He was dangerously prone to sudden but short-lived enthusiasms; he could be ruthless and selfish and, on occasion, staggeringly self-righteous; he had a deeply ingrained suspiciousness and was reluctant ever to give his confidence fully to anyone (with

LEFT: John Alexander Guy, (b. 1949). John Guy was educated at Clare College, University of Cambridge, where he studied under Sir Geoffrey Elton. Specialising chiefly in the Tudor period, his many books include *Elizabeth: The Forgotten Years* (2016), *A Daughter's Love: Thomas and Margaret More* (2008), and *'My Heart is My Own': the Life of Mary Queen of Scots* (2004). He has taught at Bristol University, The John Hopkins University and University of Rochester, and until 2002 was Professor of Modern History at the University of St Andrews. He then returned to Clare College, where he has remained. His books include *Henry VIII* in the Penguin Monarchs' series, *The Tudors: A Very Short Introduction* and *Tudor England. Courtesy John Guy*

RIGHT: David Starkey, (b. 1945). David Starkey CBE FSA FRHistS was educated at Cambridge and specialised in Tudor history, writing a thesis on King Henry VIII's household. From Cambridge he moved to the London School of Economics, where he was a lecturer in history until 1998. His numerous works include *The Reign of Henry VIII* (1985), *Six Wives: The Queens of Henry VIII* (2003) and *Henry: Virtuous Prince* (2008).

the possible exception of Cardinal Wolsey); and his devotion to pleasure, combined with his disinclination to work hard at the day-to-day business of ruling, left him wide open to manipulation by those around him. Whereas his father Henry VII had excelled in his application to routine matters of government, his son and successor:

> . . . could scarcely be bothered to look at accounts, let alone check them; he would read nothing more than a short letter, and often not even that; while writing, as he himself said, was 'to me somewhat tedious and painful'. . . None of this made him a cipher. He had secretaries and attendants to do his reading and writing for him, and councillors to cope with the detailed execution of policy and finance. But even when his whole energies were involved it put him at one removed from events: he saw and heard indeed, but through the eyes and ears of others.

The king's powerful personality, nevertheless, permeated every aspect of his reign and its politics: idle he might have been but be could never be ignored, as both Wolsey and Thomas Cromwell recognised (although both of them, in the end, also fell from grace, not least because Henry's enthusiasms, fluctuations, and irregular attention to matters of state provided an open invitation for faction to flourish both at court and in the royal council). Clearly, this Henry VIII was not the archetypal strong king but nor was he in any sense a weakling; his personality, however, certainly did provide ample scope for the politics of intrigue and faction to flourish; and it was in his handling of this that Starkey, in 1985, was perhaps at his best and most original.

By 2008, when David Starkey published *Henry: Virtuous Prince* covering Henry VIII's childhood, adolescence and early years on the throne, the historian himself had become very much a celebrity in his own right, courtesy of years of media exposure on both radio and television. Throughout, fortunately, his interest in the second Tudor monarch had never seriously flagged; on the contrary, his knowledge and understanding had expanded and deepened considerably. As a result he was now particularly anxious to stress that 'there are two Henrys' and that 'they are very different'. The Henry of his 2008 book, he emphasised, was:

> . . . a young handsome prince, slim, athletic, musical and learned as no English ruler had been for centuries. This Henry loved his mother and—most unusually for a boy at the time— was brought up with his sisters, with all that implies about the civilising and softening impact of female company. He was conventionally pious: he prostrated himself before images and showed himself profoundly respectful of the pope as head of the church. He proclaimed that 'I loved true where I did marry', and meant it. He determined to knit up the wounds of the Wars of the Roses and restore the dispossessed. He abominated his father's meanness, secrecy and corrosive mistrust. Instead, he modelled himself on Henry V, the greatest and noblest of his predecessors. Or he would be a new Arthur with a court that put Camelot in the shade.

Starkey's 'other Henry' is the mature king portrayed by Hans Holbein who, 'in his last dozen or so years', turned into:

> . . . the hulking tyrant, with a face like a Humpty Dumpty of nightmare, who broke with Rome and made himself supreme head of the church; who married six wives, of whom he divorced two and divorced and executed two others; who dissolved six hundred monasteries, demolished most of them and shattered the religious pieties and practices of a thousand years; who beheaded nobles and ministers, including those who had been his closest friends, castrated, disembowelled and quartered rebels and traitors, boiled poisoners and burned heretics.

Yet, Starkey added, this is also 'the king who reinvented England' and 'carried the powers of the English monarchy to their peak'.

2009 marked the five hundredth anniversary of Henry VIII's accession to the throne and, appropriately enough, the British Library mounted a major exhibition, guest curated by David Starkey, to celebrate so momentous an event. A handsomely produced and superbly illustrated catalogue, *Henry VIII: Man and Monarch*, edited by Oxford historian Susan Doran, contained a series of stimulating

Left: Richard Rex (b. 1961). Richard Rex was educated at Warwick School and Trinity College, Cambridge. After a brief spell in H.M. Treasury he returned to Cambridge, to write a doctorate on Bishop John Fisher, under the supervision of Brendan Bradshaw (himself once a student of Elton's). Reader in Reformation History at Cambridge, and a Fellow of Queens' College, Rex specialises in the history of the English Reformation. *Courtesy Richard Rex*

Right: Susan Doran (b. 1948). Susan was an undergraduate at St Anne's College, Oxford, and did her doctorate at University College London on the political career of Thomas Radcliffe, 3rd Earl of Sussex. She is at present a Senior Research Fellow at Jesus College, Oxford, and a Fellow and Tutor in History at St Benet's Hall, Oxford. She has written books on the foreign policy, politics, and religion of the Tudors, most recently *Elizabeth I and her Circle* (2015). *Courtesy Susan Doran*

essays by several present-day scholars of the king and his reign. It went out of its way to emphasise that the exhibition itself not only featured 'important and rarely displayed items from the British Library's unrivalled Henry VIII collection' (among them royal letters, official documents, maps and books from the king's own library) but also 'loans from other national and international museums and collections' (including weapons, armour, tapestries and portraits of the king, his family, his courtiers, his councillors and his friends). And the catalogue certainly had no difficulty at all in justifying the exhibition:

> Henry VIII is not only England's best known king, with his six wives, his girth and his bloodthirstiness. He is also one of England's most important rulers. When he came to the throne Henry was the Pious Prince who ruled an England at the heart of Catholic Europe; when he died, he was the Great Schismatic, who had created a national church and insular, xenophobic politics that shaped the development of England for the next half a millennium.

Henrician Gallery

A Portrait of Henry VIII. Black, red, and white chalk on pink-primed paper. Susan Foister, in her book *Holbein in England* suggests this drawing resembles the portrait of Henry VIII in Holbein's cartoon for a large mural at Whitehall Palace, later destroyed in a fire, and may have been copied from the mural. The right-handed shading indicates that the copy is not by Holbein himself, who was left-handed. The sheet is inscribed on the back 'Hans Swarttung', who may have been an assistant of Holbein. *State Graphics Collection, Munich.*

ABOVE LEFT: Margaret Beaufort, (1443–1509). Margaret was the daughter of Margaret Beauchamp of Bletsoe and John Beaufort, 1st Duke of Somerset. Margaret's father was a great-grandson of King Edward III through his third surviving son, John of Gaunt, Duke of Lancaster. Most surprising to modern readers is the fact that Margaret was just 13 when she gave birth to Henry, later to become King Henry VII.

ABOVE RIGHT: Henry VII, Henry Tudor, (1457–1509, king 1485–1509). Henry was the son of Edmund Tudor, 1st Earl of Richmond (1431–1456) and Margaret Beaufort, (1443–1509). Edmund Tudor was the first son of Owen Tudor and Catherine of Valois, widow of King Henry V of England, but more importantly the daughter Charles VI of France, (1368–1422).

PREVIOUS PAGE, BELOW: Elizabeth of York, queen consort to Henry VII. Elizabeth is holding the white rose of York. On 18 January 1486, some six months after Henry VII defeated her Yorkist uncle Richard III at the Battle of Bosworth, Elizabeth married Henry in Westminster Abbey. Their first son, Arthur, was born on 20 September 1486. Elizabeth of York was crowned queen on 25 November 1487. Following her coronation, she gave birth to six more children, but only four survived infancy: Margaret, Arthur, Henry (the future Henry VIII) and Mary.

ABOVE LEFT: Arthur Tudor, (1486–1502). Arthur Tudor was Prince of Wales, Earl of Chester and Duke of Cornwall. His Christian name was symbolic, with reference to the Arthur of Celtic British lore. At the age of eleven, Arthur was formally betrothed to Catherine of Aragon and after their marriage in 1501 the couple took up residence at Ludlow Castle in Shropshire, where Arthur died five months later, probably of sweating sickness.

ABOVE RIGHT: Catherine of Aragon, (1485–1536). Catherine was Queen of England from June 1509 until May 1533 as the first wife of King Henry VIII; she was previously Princess of Wales as the wife of Prince Arthur. Catherine was the daughter of Queen Isabella I of Castile and King Ferdinand II of Aragon. She was three years old when she was betrothed to Prince Arthur, and they married in 1501. In 1507, she held the position of ambassador for the Spanish Court in England. Catherine later firmly stated that the marriage to Arthur had not been consummated. She subsequently married Arthur's younger brother, the recently succeeded Henry VIII, in 1509. Portrait: Young Catherine by Michael Sittow. *Kunsthistorisches Museum, Vienna*

LEFT: Catherine of Aragon at the age of 40. In 1533 Henry declared his marriage to be invalid. Catherine refused to accept Henry as Supreme Head of the Church of England and considered herself the King's rightful wife and queen, attracting much popular sympathy. After being banished from court, she lived out the remainder of her life at Kimbolton Castle, and died there on 7 January 1536. *Reproduced from collection of the Duke of Buccleuch and Queensberry*

RIGHT: Henry VIII, a portrait dating from shortly after his coronation in 1509. Henry, who had been titled Duke of York, became the heir apparent after Arthur died and took on the title of Prince of Wales. Catherine of Aragon and Henry VIII were betrothed and later married on 11 June 1509. Catherine of Aragon and Henry VIII's marriage was a good match, not least in promoting an alliance with Spain through Catherine's nephew, the Holy Roman Emperor Charles V.

The Battle of the Spurs, 1513. Henry VIII had joined in the Holy League on 13 October 1511 with Venice and Spain to defend the Papacy from its enemies and France with military force. An initial joint Anglo-Spanish attack on Aquitaine was planned for the spring to recover it for England, but it was a failure. In 1513 Henry landed at Calais with a considerable force and the battle of Guinegate took place on 16 August 1513. English and Imperial troops under Henry VIII and Emperor Maximilian surprised and routed a body of French cavalry under Jacques de La Palice. Henry and Maximilian were besieging the town of Thérouanne in Artois (now Pas-de-Calais).

Emperor Maximilian, (1459–1519). Maximilian became well known to Henry's grandfather, Edward IV, after he married Mary of Burgundy in 1477. He became Emperor in 1486. The prolonged Italian Wars resulted in Maximilian joining the Holy League to counter the French. In 1513, with Henry VIII, Maximilian won the important victory at the battle of the Spurs against the French, stopping their advance in northern France. Portrait by Albrecht Dürer, 1519. *Kunsthistorisches Museum, Vienna*

Henry greets Emperor Maximilian. Henry's camp was at Guinegate, now called Enguinegatte. After Thérouanne fell, Henry VIII besieged and took Tournai. *The Royal Collection*

LEFT: James IV, (1473–1513) and the Battle of Flodden, 9 September 1513. Reasons for the battle are uncertain, with the common consensus being that it was probably to uphold the Auld Alliance between Scotland and France. French King Louis XII was at war with King Henry VIII and it is thought the attack by James was an attempt to divert military attention. This animosity was surprising given that James' queen was Margaret Tudor, the sister of Henry VIII. Henry was expecting an attack and ordered the Earl of Surrey to raise troops and counter the attack. It was a military disaster for the Scots. King James IV dallied for too long at his camp at Ford Castle and, as a result, he lost his advantage. By the time the opposing sides met at the battlefield, he had been outmanoeuvred by the English troops. In a single afternoon 14,000 men were slain. This number included the king, his son Alexander and a large number of Scottish nobility. *National Gallery of Scotland*

RIGHT: Margaret Tudor, (1489–1541). Margaret was the sister of Henry VIII. She was queen of Scotland 1503 until 1513 as the wife of James IV and then regent for their son James V. The crown of Scotland passed from James V to his daughter Mary, Queen of Scots, then to her son James VI. After the death of Henry VIII's daughter, Margaret's niece, Queen Elizabeth I of England, James VI inherited the throne of England in 1603 as King James I. Portrait of Margaret Tudor by Daniel Mytens.

King Francis I of France, (1494–1547, king 1515–1547). Francis was the first King of France from the Angoulême branch of the House of Valois, reigning from 1515 until his death. He was the son of Charles, Count of Angoulême, and Louise of Savoy. He succeeded his cousin and father-in-law Louis XII, who died without a male heir.

Only one year after The Field of the Cloth of Gold Francis found himself at war with both Henry and the Emperor Charles V. The latter defeated Francis at the Battle of Pavia, 24 February 1525, and Francis was captured. At the Treaty of the More, Wolsey's home in Hertfordshire, the provisional French Government signed a peace treaty with Henry, and the English undertook to assist in negotiations with Charles for the release of Francis who was held captive in Madrid. In the Treaty of Madrid, signed on 14 January 1526, Francis was forced to make major concessions to Charles V in exchange for his freedom.

Henry VIII's embarkation at Dover, 1520. A coloured engraving by James Basire, 1775 from a painting by an unknown artist, 1520–1550 commemorating Henry VIII's voyage to the Field of Cloth of Gold in 1520. *Royal Collection*

The Field of the Cloth of Gold with Henry VIII and Francis I. Unlike the majority of contemporary or near contemporary images in this book, this is a nineteenth century painting by John Gilbert (1817–1897). *Parliamentary Art Collection*

The Bakehouse. This detail from the 1545 painting shown on pages 34–35 has been chosen as it shows catering on a magnificent scale with brimming, boiling vats, roasting on spits and baking at an industrial level with a sophisticated masonry bread oven.

The Jousting Ground. Another detail from the 1545 painting, this time just a little above the bakehouse scene. The two kings with their respective queens watch a tourney taking place.

ABOVE LEFT: Sir Thomas Wyatt, (1503–1542). Wyatt was a poet and a diplomat. After taking his degree at St John's College, Cambridge, he followed in the footsteps of his father Henry Wyatt in obtaining a position at Court. In 1524 Henry VIII assigned Thomas Wyatt to be an ambassador at home and abroad and he accompanied Sir John Russell to Rome on the failed mission to petition Pope Clement VII to annul the marriage of Henry to Catherine. Black and coloured chalks, pen and ink portrait by Hans Holbein the Younger. *Royal Collection*

ABOVE RIGHT: Mary Boleyn, (*c.* 1499–1543). Mary was the sister of Anne Boleyn, probably an elder sister; she was one of Henry's mistresses between 1521 and 1526. Mary was married twice; first in 1520 to William Carey, (*c.* 1520–1528). In 1534 she married a second time, this time secretly, and to William Stafford, from a good family but with few prospects. This marriage angered both Henry and Mary's own sister, Queen Anne, and she was banished from the royal court.

RIGHT: William Carey, (*c.* 1500–1528). Carey served Henry as a Gentleman of the Privy chamber, and Esquire of the Body to the King and was widely regarded as one of the King's favourites, possibly because like the King he was fond of hunting and jousting. He distinguished himself in jousting at the Field of the Cloth of Gold in 1520 but died of the sweating sickness eight years later.

Anne Boleyn, (*c.* 1501– 1536). Anne was the daughter of Thomas Boleyn, 1st Earl of Wiltshire, and his wife, Lady Elizabeth Howard. She received some education in France where she became a maid of honour to Claude of France, daughter of Louis XII, who in 1517 became Queen of France as queen consort to Francis I. Anne returned to England in late 1521 or early 1522. It was initially planned for her to James Butler, 9th Earl of Ormond, but the plans came to nothing, possibly due to the influence of Cardinal Wolsey. Instead she secured a post at court as maid of honour to Queen Catherine. Late sixteenth-century copy of a lost original of *c.* 1533–1536. *National Portrait Gallery*

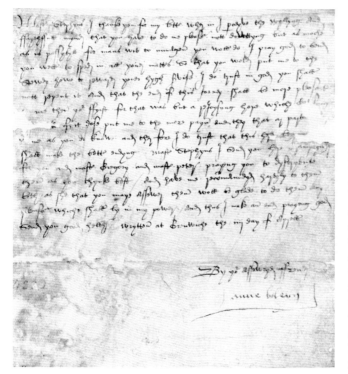

A letter from Anne Boleyn. In the early months of 1526 Henry turned his attention to Anne and began his pursuit, but she resisted his attempts to make her his mistress. Henry's absorbing desires turned into a virtual obsession and he made attempts to have his marriage to Catherine annulled. When it became clear that Pope Clement VII would not allow the marriage to be annulled, it seemed that only a break with Rome would give Henry the freedom he demanded.

Thomas Cranmer, (1489–1556). Cranmer was recruited from Cambridge by Wolsey and in 1527 he took part in an embassy to Spain. On his return from Spain the king personally interviewed him for half an hour and Cranmer described Henry as 'the kindest of princes'.

Cranmer became Archbishop of Canterbury in late 1532 and then helped to build the case for the annulment of Henry's marriage to Catherine. Along with Thomas Cromwell, he supported the principle of Royal Supremacy, whereby the king was considered sovereign over the Church within his realm. Portrait of Thomas Cranmer, c. 1545 by Gerlach Flicke, (1495–1558). *National Portrait Gallery*

The Courtship of Anne Boleyn—The Great Matter. Henry and Anne secretly married on 25 January 1533. On 23 May Cranmer declared Henry and Catherine's marriage to be null and void and, just a few days later, Henry and Anne's marriage valid. The break with Rome was now inevitable and the Pope pronounced sentences of excommunication against Henry and Cranmer. The Catholic Church in England became the Church of England with the king at its head. An 1868 painting by Emanuel Gottlieb Leutze, (1816–1868). *Smithsonian American Art Museum*

The Ambassadors. The figure on the left is Jean de Dinteville, Seigneur of Polisy, (1504–1555), French ambassador to the court of Henry VIII for most of 1533. On the right, probably, is Georges de Selve, (1509–1541), Bishop of Lavaur. This painting has been the topic of much discussion and speculation over the years with so many symbolic features resulting in conflicting interpretations. Painting by Hans Holbein the Younger, c. 1533. *National Gallery, London*

The Skull. The most notable feature in the Ambassadors is the distorted skull rendered in anamorphic perspective, an invention of the Early Renaissance. When viewed from immediately below, its perspective becomes obvious.

Study for the Family Portrait of Thomas More. Pen and brush in black on top of chalk. This is a preparatory sketch for Holbein's portrait of the family of Thomas More, now lost, thought to be the first life-sized group portrait north of the Alps. The painted work was copied several times though differences between the copies and this sketch suggest that intervening versions may have existed. The astronomer Nicholas Kratzer, (1487–1550), a friend of Holbein and More, and the tutor of More's children, added the names and ages of the sitters in Latin on the sketch in brown ink. On the left is Elizabeth Dauncy, More's second daughter; beside her is his adopted daughter, Margaret Giggs, explaining a point to Thomas More's father, John More; Thomas More himself sits in the centre, with the engaged couple Anne Cresacre and his only son, John More, on either side of him; beside John More is the household fool, Henry Patenson; on the right of the picture are More's youngest daughter, Cecily Heron, and his eldest daughter, Margaret Roper; More's second wife, Alice, is kneeling on the extreme right. *Kupferstichkabinett, Öffentliche Kunstsammlung, Basel*

Sir Thomas More and Family, after Hans Holbein the Younger. Sir Thomas More was executed in 1535 for his opposition to Henry VIII's religious reforms. This painting survives in many copies, some varying quite widely. This particular copy is of interest, as unlike many other versions, it has a portrait of Queen Mary hanging on the wall, and extra characters have been added to the right wearing ruff collars, which did not come into fashion much before 1570. This leads to the conclusion that this version was painted for, or belonged to, a recusant family, most probably from the north of England.

Anne Boleyn's Final Days. Anne was crowned on 1 June 1533 and on 7 September she gave birth to Elizabeth. Three miscarriages followed and, by March 1536, Henry was courting Jane Seymour. It is doubtful if any new source will come to light but historical speculation suggests that Anne's fall and execution were engineered by Thomas Cromwell. Henry had Anne investigated for high treason in April 1536 and on 2 May she was arrested and sent to the Tower of London, where she was tried before a jury of peers which included her own uncle, Thomas Howard. She was found guilty on 15 May and beheaded four days later. Anne Boleyn Says a Final Goodbye to her Daughter, an 1838 painting by Gustav Vappers, (1803–1874).

The Pilgrimage of Grace. Northern rebellions had been a problem for Henry's grandfather, Edward IV, and Henry experienced similar unrest in 1536 and 1537. The rising began on 2 October 1536 at Louth, the stated reason being the suppression of monasteries and priories, and quickly gained ground throughout Lincolnshire, prompted by Roman Catholics against the establishment of the Church of England. Contagion spread to Yorkshire where their leader, Robert Aske led 9,000 rebels into York. Eventually Aske's followers numbered more than 40,000.

The Duke of Norfolk eventually regained control and Aske and many others were executed, but it was a deeply troubling time for Henry. The Beginning of the Pilgrimage of Grace Lincoln, by Andrew Benjamin Donaldson. *Art & Archaeology in Lincolnshire*

Jane Seymour, (*c.* 1508–1537). Jane had been a maid of honour to Queen Catherine and went on to serve Queen Anne. Clearly, Henry's roving eye had observed Jane at court and his desires, coupled with his quest for a male heir and reinforced by Anne's miscarriages, formed a justification in his mind for becoming betrothed to Jane on 20 May 1536, just one day after Anne's execution. They were married four days later. On 12 October 1537 Jane gave birth to the long-awaited male heir at Hampton Court Palace. The birth had been difficult, labour lasting two nights and three days, and Jane Seymour died on 24 October 1537 from complications associated with the birth. *Kunsthistorisches Museum*

Prince Edward as a young child. The Latin translates as: *Little one, emulate thy father and be the heir of his virtue; the world contains nothing greater. Heaven and earth could scarcely produce a son whose glory would surpass that of such a father. Do thou but equal the deeds of thy parent and men can ask no more. Shouldst thou surpass him, thou hast outstript all, nor shall any surpass thee in ages to come. By Sir Richard Morison.* A portrait by Hans Holbein the Younger. *The National Gallery of Art, Washington, D.C.*

Hampton Court. Thomas Wolsey took over the site of Hampton Court in 1514; it had previously been a property of the Order of St John of Jerusalem. Over a seven year period Wolsey spent a vast sum to create one of the finest palaces in England of that time. Henry VIII stayed in the state apartments as Wolsey's guest immediately after their completion in 1525.

A Game of Real Tennis. The game evolved in France and royal interest in England began with Henry V. It was Henry VIII who made the biggest impact as a young monarch, playing the game with gusto at Hampton Court on a court he built after he had effectively 'purloined' the palace.

The Entrance to the Tennis Court. Wolsey, sensing the mood at the time, gifted the palace to Henry in 1528. Two years later Henry had an inside tennis court built where he enjoyed the sport with favourites such as Thomas Wyatt. Anne Boleyn was watching a game of real tennis when she was arrested and Henry is said to have been playing tennis when news of her execution was brought to him.

Henry and Jousting. Along with tennis and hunting, another favourite pastime was jousting. On 10 March 1524 Henry suffered a jousting accident after he forgot to lower his visor in a joust against Charles Brandon. A more serious accident occurred at a tournament at Greenwich Palace on 24 January 1536 when Henry, in full armour, was thrown from his horse, itself armoured, which then fell on top of him. He was unconscious for two hours and was thought at first to have been fatally injured. This manuscript illustration shows Henry jousting with Catherine of Aragon looking on.

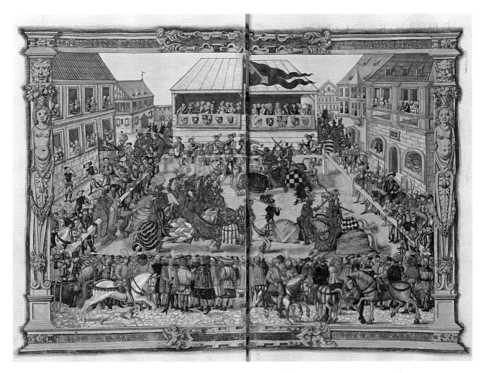

Feet Planted in the Middle Ages. A frequent jousting as well as tennis partner was the court favourite, and poet, Thomas Wyatt. Although both were Renaissance men, they had feet planted in the Middle Ages as well; as for chivalric tournaments and jousting, whilst outdated from a military perspective, they still remained fashionable in courtly circles. The above depiction is a feat of arms tournament in Worms in 1487 by Jörg Breu the Younger. *Bayerische Staatsbibliothek, Munich*

Anne of Cleves, (1515–1557). Hans Holbein was sent to paint Anne at Düren in the summer of 1539, to enable Henry to judge whether she was appropriate match. Hans Holbein the Younger, c. 1539. *Louvre Museum*

The Meeting on New Years' Day 1540. Henry decided to get an early glimpse of his new bride and went to Rochester where she was staying *en route* to London from Dover. Henry and Anne met officially two days later at Greenwich Park, where a grand reception had been prepared for her. The couple were married on 6 January 1540; on 24 June Anne was commanded to leave the Court; and on 6 July she was informed of her husband's decision to render their marriage annulled. Henry confided to Cromwell that he had not consummated the marriage, saying, 'I liked her before not well, but now I like her much worse.' He described her as having unpleasant body odour and sagging breasts, among other complaints. Redesignated as 'king's sister', she remained in England where she died during the reign of Queen Mary. Cromwell's failure to prevent the marriage without disrupting an important German ally was a great irritation to Henry and, indeed, instrumental in bringing about his downfall.

LEFT: Portrait of a Lady. This miniature is generally considered to be Catherine Howard, (*c.* 1521–1542). Catherine was a niece of Thomas Howard, 3rd Duke of Norfolk, (1473–1554), and Norfolk took advantage of the situation when Henry made it clear in the spring of 1540 that he preferred Catherine to his new German bride. Norfolk organised a coup against Cromwell and had him arrested at a stormy Privy Council meeting—obviously with Henry's acquiescence. In his anger and frustration the king had finally turned on Cromwell to his subsequent regret. Cromwell's enemies—Norfolk at the forefront—had long waited for him to make his first mistake. Miniature *c.* 1540 by Hans Holbein the Younger. *Royal Collection*

RIGHT: Catherine Howard's Downfall, November 1541. It was alleged that earlier in the year she had embarked upon a romance with Henry's favourite courtier, Thomas Culpeper. Witnesses to her indiscretions asked for favours in return for silence, and many were appointed to her household. At the urging of the Dowager Duchess of Norfolk, Catherine appointed Francis Dereham as her personal secretary. This miscalculation led to the charges of treason and adultery against her. It came to light that in 1538 when Catherine was in the Dowager Duchess's household she had had a relationship with Dereham. They had become lovers there, even addressing each other as 'husband' and 'wife'. Establishing the existence of a pre-contract between Catherine and Dereham would have had the effect of terminating Catherine's royal union, but it also would have allowed Henry to annul their marriage and banish her from Court. Catherine would have been disgraced, impoverished, and exiled, but, she would have been spared the axe. Instead she denied any pre-contract, claiming that Dereham had raped her. Her situation was made more complicated by the revelation of her affair with Culpeper. Culpeper and Dereham were executed at Tyburn on 10 December 1541, Catherine was executed on 13 February 1542. An engraving by Wenceslaus Hollar (1607–1677) after Holbein. *Thomas Fisher Rare Book Library*

Henry Howard Earl of Surrey, (1517–1547). The fate of Henry Howard seems strange and sad for a person of such talent. He and his friend Sir Thomas Wyatt were the first English poets to write in the sonnet form that Shakespeare later used. Surrey was a brave, though sometimes foolhardy military leader; he won Henry's approval during various military campaigns, only to forfeit it through imprudence and the loss of many men in a skirmish. He was eventually convicted of treason on rather dubious grounds related to his armorial bearings. His downfall is not easy to understand but may have been the result of paranoia on Henry VIII's part as he became convinced that Surrey planned to usurp the crown from his son Edward. Henry had Surrey sentenced to death on 13 January 1547 and he was beheaded for treason on 19 January 1547.

Thomas Howard, 3rd Duke of Norfolk, (1473–1554). Norfolk, uncle of Anne Boleyn and Catherine Howard, was a prominent member of Henry's council. He had secured victory over King James of Scotland at Flodden and had been a successful Lord Deputy in Ireland. He was opposed to the new ministers favoured by Henry whom he believed to be encroaching on noble prerogatives. With this belief he was an enemy first of Wolsey, then, of Wolsey's protégé Thomas Cromwell. Norfolk hoped to be promoted to become Henry's closest minister after his successful management of the military campaign against the Pilgrimage of Grace, but Cromwell continued as Henry's chief minister. During the 1530s he and Cromwell strongly competed for position, and Norfolk eventually gained the upper hand when Cromwell failed to find an exit route for Henry in regard to Anne of Cleves. Norfolk came to grief himself, when his son, Henry Howard, Earl of Surrey was accused of treason, and Norfolk spent the whole of the reign of Edward VI in the Tower, before being released on Mary's accession, aged eighty.

The Tower of London. The White Tower, which gives its name to the entire castle was built by William the Conqueror in 1078. There were several phases of expansion but, by the late thirteenth century and despite later activity on the site, the Tower had grown into the form in which it is now seen. A view from the South Bank looking towards the Traitor's Gate.

The Tower from a Fifteenth Century Manuscript. A depiction of the imprisonment of Charles, Duke of Orléans, in the Tower of London from a fifteenth-century manuscript. Although several decades before Henry's time, the scene would have changed little. Beyond the Tower, Lower Key, Billingsgate and London Bridge are clearly depicted. *British Library, MS Royal, 16 folio 73*

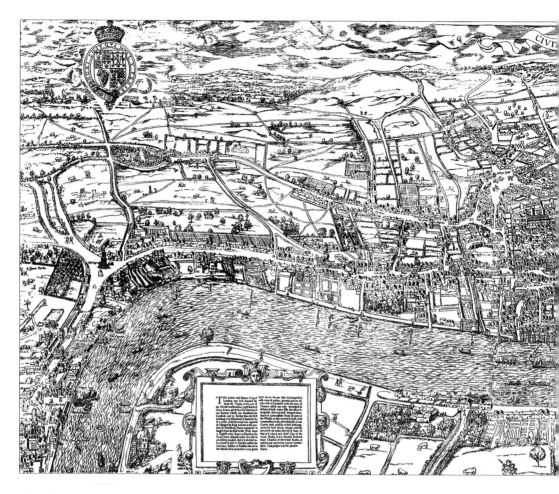

Top: The Map of London, 1560. This map was long upheld to be the work of Ralph Agas (c. 1540 – 26 November 1621), but this attribution is now believed to be incorrect. The map provides a dramatic depiction of the layout of Henry's London. The area between Holborn and Westminster was virtually rural at that time.

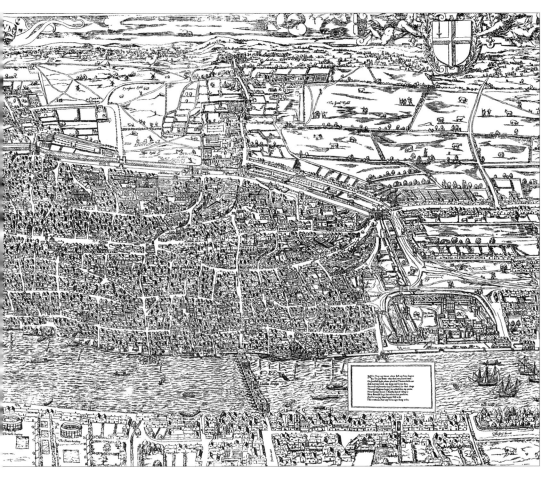

ABOVE: The Visscher Panorama of London in 1616. This fine panorama makes an appropriate accompaniment to the map. It is an engraving by Dutch mapmaker and publisher Claes Janszoon Visscher (1587–1652).

ABOVE: London Bridge *c.* 1650. The buildings here were probably much as in Tudor times. This medieval bridge and its Saxon predecessor remained based on original Roman piers. Painting by Claude de Jongh. *English Heritage*

Charles V, (1500–1558) as a Young Man with his Famous Habsburg Jaw, *c.* 1520. Charles was the grandson of Henry's earlier ally Maximilian and, following the deaths of his grandfathers, Ferdinand and Maximilian, in 1516 and 1519 respectively, Charles ascended the throne of Spain and was also elected to succeed his Habsburg grandfather, Maximilian I, as Holy Roman Emperor. In 1521 Charles allied himself with Henry against Francis I of France, resulting in a small English army attacking in the north of France, but the campaign made little progress. Charles V, on the other hand, was successful and defeated and captured Francis at Pavia enabling Charles to dictate the peace terms; however, he believed he owed Henry nothing. Sensing Charles' indifference, Henry took England out of the war, signing the Treaty of the More on 30 August 1525. A portrait by Bernard van Orley, (*c.* 1492–1542). *Museum of Fine Arts, Budapest*

Portrait of Charles V with Beard, Probably
Grown to Disguise the Jaw. Charles' relations
with Henry seriously deteriorated when Henry
divorced Charles' aunt Catherine. When Charles
and Francis made peace in January 1539, Henry
became increasingly paranoid, perhaps as a result
of receiving a constant list of threats to the kingdom
supplied by Cromwell in his role as spymaster. In
1539 the alliance between Francis and Charles fell
apart and degenerated into renewed war. With
Catherine of Aragon and Anne Boleyn dead,
relations between Charles and Henry improved.
Henry now concluded a secret alliance with the
Emperor and decided to enter the war against
Francis. Henry finally went to France in June 1544
but, to Charles' annoyance, he did not march on
Paris. Charles' own campaign lacked success and
he made peace once more with Francis leaving
Henry in the lurch to conclude his own settlement.
A portrait attributed to Lambert Sustris, (1515–1591).
Alte Pinakothek, Munich

Catherine Parr, (1512–1548). Catherine was twice widowed and in 1543, using her late mother's friendship with Catherine of Aragon, she took the opportunity to renew her own friendship with Henry's VIII's daughter Mary. By February 1543 Catherine had established herself as part of Mary's household and it was there that she caught the attention of the king. Catherine married Henry VIII on 12 July 1543 at Hampton Court Palace. Anonymous portrait. *Lord Hastings, Seaton Delaval, Norfolk*

KATHARINE PARRE

Catherine Parr. Catherine enjoyed a close relationship with Henry's three children and was personally involved in the education of Elizabeth and Edward. She was influential in Henry's passing of the Third Succession Act in 1543 that restored both his daughters, Mary and Elizabeth, to the line of succession to the throne. Six months after Henry's death, she married her fourth and final husband, Thomas Seymour, 1st Baron Seymour of Sudeley. Catherine died in September 1548, probably from complications in childbirth. Anonymous portrait *c.* 1545. *National Portrait Gallery*

A Tudor Funeral Procession Preceded by the Heralds. This illustration is from 1603 depicting the funeral procession for Henry's daughter Elizabeth I. The ritual and procession would have been similar for Henry. Tudor funerals had a strongly heraldic flavour and those taking part in the procession would generally have been noblemen wearing full-length black mourning cloaks and hoods, as did their attendants. The quality and amount of material in these garments was strictly regulated by the College of Arms, according to the rank of the wearer.

Edward VI and the Pope: An Allegory of the Reformation. This propaganda painting was probably produced between 1568 and 1571 to commemorate the anti-papal policies of Edward VI and celebrate the successful re-establishment of the Church of England under Elizabeth. Henry VIII is on his deathbed and his son Edward is seated beneath a cloth of state with a slumping pope at his feet. At Edward's side are his uncle the Lord Protector Edward Seymour, and members of the Privy Council including John Russell, 1st Earl of Bedford, Thomas Cranmer, and John Dudley, Duke of Northumberland. *National Portrait Gallery*

The cortège for Elizabeth I, 1603. The horse-drawn bier is flanked, as in modern times, by Gentlemen-pensioners carrying their axes 'reversed'. The coffin has an effigy of the late Queen on top of it, and is flanked by knights holding banners and a canopy. In the fifteenth and sixteenth centuries it became customary for a lifelike wax effigy of the deceased sovereign to be carried on or near the coffin in royal funeral processions. The last effigy of a monarch to be carried in procession was that of James I in 1625.

Edward VI, (born 1537, king 1547–1553). The household established around Edward was, at first, under Sir William Sidney, and later Sir Richard Page. Henry demanded exacting standards of security and cleanliness in his son's household, stressing that Edward was 'this whole realm's most precious jewel'. Edward was a tall and merry child. Despite occasional illnesses and poor eyesight he enjoyed good health until the last six months of his life.

Edward VI Inherited the Tudor Red Hair. The red hair probably came from his grandmother, Elizabeth of York, and great-grandmother Elizabeth Woodville. The medieval standard for beauty was red-gold hair, so Edward and Elizabeth, his half-sister, conformed to fashion. Edward also followed fashion with his hair cropped short. Both Edward's sisters were attentive to their brother and often visited him. In 1543, Henry invited his children to spend Christmas with him, indicating his reconciliation with his daughters, the work of his new wife Catherine Parr, of whom Edward soon became fond. Miniature, possibly by William Scrots. *Metropolitan Museum of Art*

Accession of Edward VI. Edward succeeded his father on 28 January 1547 under a council initially led by his uncle Edward Seymour, 1st Duke of Somerset, (1547–1549). The transformation of the Church occurred under Edward, who took an interest in religious matters. Henry VIII, had severed the link with Rome, but never permitted the renunciation of Catholic doctrine or ceremony. It was during Edward's reign that Protestantism was established, clerical celibacy was abolished and the services were rendered in English. In early 1553 Edward fell ill and after several months of incapacity he died on 6 July 1553 at the age of 15. His death may have been tuberculosis, but one other theory is bronchopneumonia. Henry's dream of a male heir succeeding, and reaching maturity had come to an end.

The Prince Regent Visits the Vault. George, Prince of Wales, caricatured in 'Amongst the Tombs', by George Cruikshank, 1813. After he was made Prince Regent in 1811, the future George IV began to develop projects that would enhance his status as royal ruler. One such project was the construction of a new burial vault in St George's Chapel. In 1813, during the excavation work for a passageway leading to this vault, workmen accidentally uncovered the tombs of Kings Henry VIII and Charles I. The Prince Regent instructed the royal physician, Sir Henry Halford, to examine the tombs and conduct an autopsy on the body of Charles I.

The Vaults at St George's Chapel, Windsor. This sketch was made by Alfred Young Nutt, Surveyor to the Dean and Canons of St George's Chapel, Windsor Castle. The vault had been opened previously in 1813 and several relics removed. In 1888, under the supervision of the Prince of Wales, the future Edward VII, these relics were replaced and some measurements made. Alfred Nutt recorded that Henry VIII's coffin was about two metres in length and was in a state of disrepair with some bodily remains visible. From left to right, the coffins of Charles I, Henry VIII and Jane Seymour. On the top of King Charles' coffin, at the foot, is the tiny coffin of one of Queen Anne's five children—none of whom survived childhood. *Royal Collection*

Select Bibliography

Baker, K. (ed), *The Faber Book of English History in Verse* (1988)

Brewer, J. S., Gairdner, J., and Brodie, R. H. (eds), *Letters and Papers, Foreign and Domestic, of the Reign of Henry VIII* (21 vols, 1862–1932)

Cook, D. (ed), *Documents and Debates: Sixteenth Century England 1450–1600* (1980)

Dockray, K., 'Edward IV and Henry VIII: A Yorkist Grandfather and Tudor Grandson Compared', *Medieval History*, NS, Vol. 1 ii (2002) pp 76-83

Doran, S. (ed), *Henry VIII: Man and Monarch* (2009)

Elton, G. R., *England under the Tudors* (1955)

Elton, G. R., *Henry VIII: An Essay in Revision* (Historical Association Pamphlet, 1962)

Elton, G. R., *The Sources of History: England 1200–1640* (1969)

Elton, G. R., *Reform and Reformation: England 1509–1558* (1977)

Frazier, N. L., *English History in Contemporary Poetry: The Tudor Monarchy 1485–1588* (Historical Association pamphlet, 1914)

Guy, J., *Tudor England* (1988)

Hay, D. (ed), *The Anglica Historia of Polydore Vergil 1485–1537* (1950)

Kenyon, J., *The History Men: The Historical Profession in England since the Renaissance* (1983)

Kinghorn, A. M., *The Chorus of History: Literary-historical relations in Renaissance Britain 1485–1558* (1971)

Loades, D. (ed), *Chronicles of the Tudor Kings 1485–1553* (1996)

Morris, C., *The Tudors* (1955)

Palmer, M. D., *Henry VIII* (1971)

Pollard, A. F., *Henry VIII* (1902)

Rex, R., *The Tudors* (2002)

Ridley, J., *Henry VIII* (1984)

Routh, C. R. N. (ed), *They Saw it Happen: Eye-witness Accounts of Events in Britush History 1485–1688* (1956)

Saccio, P., *Shakespeare's English Kings* (1977)

Scarisbrick, J., *Henry VIII* (1968)

Starkey, D., *The Reign of Henry VIII* (1985)

Starkey, D., *Henry: Virtuous Prince* (2008)

Steele, R. (ed), *King's Letters: From the Early Tudors: With the Letters of Henry VIII and Anne Boleyn* (1904)

Sylvester, R. S. and Harding, D. P. (eds), *Two Early Tudor Lives: The Life and Death of Cardinal Wolsey by George Cavendish and The Life of Sir Thomas More by William Roper* (1962)

Whibley, C. (ed), *Edward Hall's Chronicle: Henry VIII*, 2 vols (1904)

Williams, C. H. (ed), *England under the Early Tudors 1485–1529* (1925)

Williams, C. H. (ed), *English Historical Documents 1485–1558* (1967)